A penetrating look into the person and work of Jesus Christ

THE ROOT & BRANCH

JOSEPH A. PIPA, Jr.

Christian Focus
Publications Ltd.

ISBN 1-871676-16-9

Printed in USA

Published under licensing agreement by
Christian Focus Publications
Geanies House, Fearn, Tain, Ross-shire IV20 1TW, Scotland

Table of Contents

FOREWORD

The apostle Paul once wrote that his great ambition in life was to know Christ (Phil. 3:10). It is an aspiration worthy of being emulated by all of us, for the Christian faith—morally, spiritually, intellectually—has Jesus Christ himself at its center. He is everything.

Yet, despite this, Christ is not always given his rightful place in the church. Much of our preaching, teaching and evangelism concentrates only on man and his need and has all too little to say about Christ and his work. Whether as a cause of this, or its effect, reliable books about Christ are not numerous. Other, and lesser, themes tend to dominate the shelves of our local Christian bookstores. As a consequence, sadly, many of us can speak articulately about our professional work, our knowledge of music and the arts, or sport, yet only with great inadequacy about our Savior. This ought not to be.

Thankfully, Joseph A. Pipa's *The Root & Branch of David* should help to supply the remedy for this situation, by its careful and richly biblical exposition of Christ and his work.

To those who know him, Dr. Pipa needs no recommendation from me. Suffice it to say that he combines to a high degree a grasp of the intellectual content of the Christian faith with a model pastoral spirit. He would be embarrassed were I to list the many complimentary things I could say about him as I have come to know and observe him in the various contexts of his family and church life, in his scholarly activities and in his denominational activities. He is a highly prized friend, especially to those who know him best.

I commend *The Root & Branch of David*. It is a full and excellent introduction to what the Bible has to say about Christ. To do you the most good, it should be read carefully, thoughtfully and prayer-fully. Approach it in this spirit and you will find much here that will show you what Paul so beautifully calls "the unsearchable riches of Christ."

Sinclair B. Ferguson
Westminster Theological Seminary
Philadelphia, Pennsylvania

Abbreviations

Reference is made in this book to what are commonly known as the Westminster Standards. These are identified as follows:

WCF the Westminster Confession of Faith
by chapter and section
For example: WCF, 8.2

SC the Shorter Catechism
by question/answer
For example: SC, Q/A 28

LC the Larger Catechism
by question/answer
For example: LC, Q/A 53

1

THE ROOT AND BRANCH OF DAVID

"Good morning, Bill. How are you doing today?"

"Pretty good, Pastor, considering what happened last Saturday."

"I imagine it was a frightening experience to come that close to death."

"Yes, it was. At first I thought I had a bad case of indigestion. But as the pain began shooting down my arm, I figured I was having a heart attack. The Lord was gracious, though. The medics were at my house with an ambulance ten minutes after I called. I thank the Lord they were there when my heart stopped. Their quick work saved my life."

"Were you conscious the whole time?"

"After they resuscitated me, I was. And that was probably the most incredible part of the whole experience."

"What do you mean?"

"Well, as I rode in the ambulance to the hospital, this awful panic and fear of dying crept over me like a dark fog. I had never known terror like that, even in Vietnam."

"What happened?"

"Well, the Lord brought to my mind a number of things that we had been studying recently in our Sunday school class about Jesus Christ. At first, all I could think about was my sins. I had an awful dread of standing before a holy God, and being cast into hell. Although I remembered that Christ suffered and died in my place and that all my sins had been forgiven, my conscience still accused me about my unworthiness. What reason did I have to think God would really accept me? Then the Holy Spirit caused me to remember the perfect righteousness that God had given me on the basis of Christ's active obedience.

"But Satan really began to press the attack: Why did I think Christ could save me? How could something that happened to an obscure Jewish man two thousand years ago help me die with confidence? I remembered learning, though, that Jesus of Nazareth is both God and man, and that he is the all-sufficient Savior.

"Satan suggested that I had no way of knowing that those things revealed in the gospel were true. He suggested that Jesus Christ was only a figment of the imaginations of men. But I remembered the testimony of the Bible—both the Old and New Testaments—about who Christ is and what he has done. At last my fears subsided. The attack was over.

"You know, Pastor, there have been times when I questioned the value of studying doctrine, but this ordeal has helped me to see its practical importance. I wish every Christian could study about the person and work of Christ as we have."

This book is about the Lord Jesus Christ, the Son of God, our Savior. Its purpose is to enable each one of us to know the Savior better so that we might more fully enjoy the grace and comfort of the gospel, and be equipped to serve the Lord in holiness.

The Messiah Comes

It was the climactic day of Simeon's life! This elderly saint was one of the godly men and women "waiting for the consolation of Israel" (Luke 2:25). God had revealed to him that he would not die before he saw the Messiah (vs. 26). On this particular day, as he entered the temple, the Spirit of God made known to him that the baby being dedicated at that time was the promised Savior. What joy Simeon felt as he took the baby in his arms and praised God for sending the long-awaited Redeemer! Simeon was joined by the prophetess Anna, who also gave thanks to God and "spoke about the child to all who were looking forward to the redemption of Jerusalem" (vs. 38).

Notice that Simeon and Anna, who had the privilege of recognizing Jesus the Savior, were part of a class of people longing for the advent of the Messiah (vs. 38). Their longing was not merely a pious hope, but rather a conviction that the time was at hand for the coming of the Savior. On the basis of Old Testament prophecy, these people were looking for the Messiah to come in their generation.

This fact ought not surprise us. The Old Testament says a great deal about the Messiah. In this chapter we will trace two important strands of Old Testament teaching about the person of the Messiah.

The Person of the Messiah

The Bible uses two unusual titles to describe the Messiah. In Isaiah 11:1 he is called "the shoot and Branch of Jesse," while in Revelation 22:16 the apostle John calls him "The Root of David." Apparently he who sprang from the root stock of David (the shoot and branch of Jesse) is in effect the root and origin of David. These apparently contradictory terms are figures of speech revealing the Messiah to be no ordinary person. He is both God and man. Let's look closely at the terms *branch* and *root* and see what important information they give us about him.

The Branch

The Savior is called "the Branch of Jesse" to signify that he was to be a descendant of David, a man who would sit on David's throne. But his family tree goes back to Adam and Eve (see Figure 1).

The first reference to the Savior is in Genesis 3:15. There we learn that there will be two lines of people on the earth. The seed or offspring of the serpent is the unrighteous line developing through Cain, and the seed or offspring of the woman is the righteous line developing through Seth (see Genesis 4:25, 26). In the conflict between the seed of Satan and the seed of the woman, the righteous line will have a champion, a particular descendant who will defeat the devil and deliver God's people. When God says to Satan, "He [the seed] shall bruise you [Satan] on the head and you shall bruise him on the heel" (Genesis 3:15), God is promising to provide a deliverer who will defeat Satan but in so doing will himself suffer.

The Messiah therefore will be a man descended from Eve through Seth. Seth is the first branch in the Savior's family tree.

The second major branch in the Messiah's family tree is Shem. Following Ham's sin, God cursed Canaan and blessed Shem (Genesis 9:26, 27). The Scripture shows that Shem was to be the father of the messianic people. In other words, the Messiah was to be a man who would come from a particular subdivision of the race of men, the Shemites.

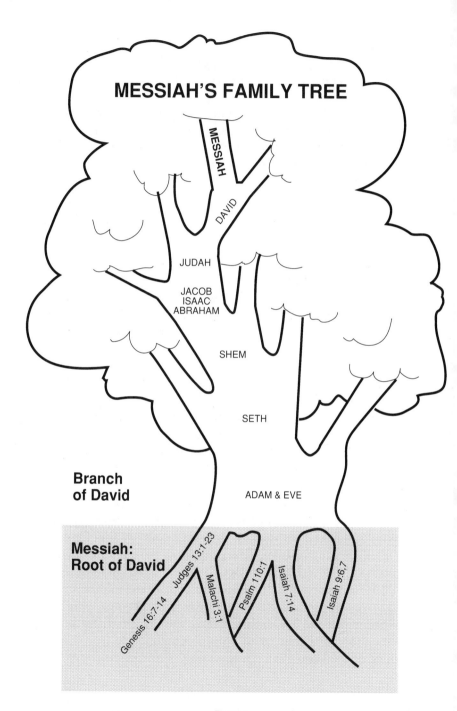

Figure 1

The next branch in the Messiah's family tree is Abraham, a descendant of Shem. God said to him,

"I will make you into a great nation and I will bless you; I will make your name great, and you will be a blessing. I will bless those who bless you, and whoever curses you I will curse; and all peoples on earth will be blessed through you" (Genesis 12:2, 3).

God makes the promise more specific in Genesis 22:18: "And through your offspring [seed] all nations on earth will be blessed, because you have obeyed me."

This promise to Abraham was repeated both to Isaac and Jacob. The promise, first given in vague and general terms, is increasingly made more specific. As the Old Testament progresses, the genealogical chart of the Savior becomes more full and detailed.

The next major subdivision of the family tree is revealed in the deathbed words of Jacob, in Egypt. He predicts that the rule of God shall not depart from Judah nor the ruler's staff from between his feet until Shiloh comes (Genesis 49:8–10, NASV). *Shiloh* means "the prince of peace" and is a title of the Messiah. The tribe of Judah is to be the ruling family and the Messiah would descend from it.

Next, God gives the privilege of rule to a specific household in Judah (2 Samuel 7:8–16). He promises that David's son will be king forever. This promise is partially fulfilled in Solomon, through whom God began a dynasty for David. Solomon, the prince of peace, built a house for the Lord. However, the perfect fulfillment of this promise was not Solomon but the Messiah—Shiloh, the Prince of Peace, the descendant of David who would establish the true, living house of the Lord God.

All Israel believed that the Messiah was to be the son of David. For this reason Matthew begins his gospel, "A record of the genealogy of Jesus Christ the Son of David, the Son of Abraham" (Matthew 1:1). As surely as a member of the Daughters of the American Revolution can trace her family tree to prove she had an ancestor in the Revolutionary War, so Jesus of Nazareth could trace his to prove he is the promised Savior, the Messiah, the descendant of David who was to rule over God's people.

The Root

The Messiah, however, was to be more than a descendant of David. That's why in retrospect the apostle John adds that he is the Root of David. In other words, he was the one from whom David had his origin (see Figure 1). Jesus Christ is also God, and therefore David's creator. This is the great mystery that Jesus used to stump the Jews, as recorded in Matthew 22:41–46: If the Messiah is to be David's son, why does David call him by the divine title Adonai (Lord)? With this question Jesus alerted the Jews that the Messiah would be more than a man. In some way he was to be divine.

In the Old Testament there are many intimations of the plurality of the Godhead. One of the principal names of God, "Elohim," is plural but is used with singular verbs. This, at least, hints at the possibility of plurality in the Godhead. We find a further intimation of plurality when Elohim says, "Let *us* make man in *our* image" (Genesis 1:26). Apparently something about God embraces plurality as well as unity.

The first clear Old Testament statement on the plurality of the Godhead is the revelation of the Angel of the Lord. The term *angel* in the Bible means "messenger." Admittedly, the word is most often used of the class of created spirits who serve God, but the Hebrew word can also be translated "messenger" and used of men (as in Haggai 1:13). So the root meaning of *Angel of the Lord* is "messenger of the Lord." The specific meaning depends on the context.

Genesis 16:7–14 tells about the appearance of the Angel of the Lord to Hagar. The angel mentioned here is clearly a unique messenger. He is sent from the Lord, but at the same time he claims divine prerogatives, for he says, "I will so increase your descendants that they will be too numerous to count" (Genesis 16:10). Only God can promise to multiply one's descendants in this way! The messenger doesn't say, "The Lord has told me to tell you . . ." He doesn't say, "The Lord, through me, guarantees to you . . ." He says, "I will increase your descendants."

Furthermore, Hagar was aware she had seen God. "She gave this name to the LORD who spoke to her: 'You are the God who sees me,' for she said, 'I have now seen the One who sees me'" (vs. 13). In some mysterious way, the one sent from God *is* God. The apostle makes a similar statement in John 1:1: "[He] was with God, and he was God."

You may ask, "What is the relationship between the Angel of the Lord and the Messiah?" The answer to this question is found in Malachi 3:1. The Angel of the Lord is going to come as the Messiah. "'See, I will send my messenger [my angel], who will prepare the way before me. Then suddenly the Lord you are seeking will come to his temple; the messenger [angel] of the covenant, whom you desire, will come,' says the LORD Almighty." The Messiah was to be the Angel of the Lord.

Keeping in mind what we have learned about the Angel of the Lord, we should not be surprised to discover a number of passages asserting the deity of the coming Messiah. We have already mentioned Matthew 22:41–46, the passage with which Jesus stumped the Jews. Basically Jesus was saying, "We all agree that the Messiah is to be the son of David, but if the Messiah is the son of David, why does David address him as Lord [Adonai]?" Jesus is referring to Psalm 110:1, where David, by inspiration, understood that in some mysterious way the Messiah was going to be divine as well as human.

But it was left to Isaiah to show most clearly the deity of the Messiah. In Chapter 7:14, he tells us that the promised seed of David was to be miraculously provided—born of a virgin—and implies that God was to be his Father: his name *Immanuel* means "God with us." In 9:6, 7 the prophet tells us that the Messiah will be "Mighty God" and "Everlasting Father." The one who is the son of David, who will sit forever on the throne of David, is in fact God. The Messiah is not only the Branch of David but also the Root of David, God as well as man.

Thus, we see that the Old Testament gives us much information about the coming Messiah. Christianity was no new thing. In the rest of this book we shall continue to explore the person and work of the Messiah. As we study what the Scriptures teach about who Jesus Christ is and what he does, we will begin to appreciate more fully the redemption he provides for his people.

Review Questions

1. What does it mean that the Messiah was the Branch of Jesse?

2. Trace the Messiah's family tree as it is revealed in the Old Testament.

3. What does it mean that the Messiah was the Root of David?

4. Demonstrate that the Angel of the Lord is God.

5. Give some Old Testament passages that prove the deity of the Messiah.

6. According to the Old Testament, when was the Messiah to come?

Discussion Questions

1. What is your reaction to discovering that the Old Testament says so much about the Savior?

2. Were any of the Old Testament prophecies that were covered in the lesson *not* fulfilled in the person and work of the Lord Jesus Christ?

3. Using the lesson material, prepare a presentation that would seek to prove to a Jew that Jesus of Nazareth is the Messiah.

4. How important is the Old Testament to Christians?

2

WHAT'S IN A NAME?

About the year A.D. 319, the church was rocked by the teaching of a minister named Arius. Arius taught that the Son of God could not be coeternal with the Father. He must, therefore, have come into existence sometime before the creation, by the creative word of the Father. Thus he was the Son of God; but he was not eternal, nor was he equal with the Father.

Because the church had not given mature reflection to what the Bible says about the deity of the Son, initially a number of people were deceived by Arius' teaching. For awhile it appeared that Christendom would adopt this erroneous view.

God, however, raised up a defender of the truth, a man named Athanasius. Athanasius suffered greatly for his views, but in A.D. 325 the Council of Nicea vindicated his position and adopted a creed that sets forth what continues to this day to be the orthodox position of the Christian church concerning the deity of the Lord Jesus Christ. (For the text of the Nicene Creed, see Appendix A).

In Chapter 1 we learned that Jesus Christ is the Branch and the Root of David—both David's descendant and David's Lord. We traced his family tree, and we also found evidence that he is more than a man: he is divine. A careful student of the Old Testament should have been prepared for John's startling declaration, "In the beginning was the Word, and the Word was with God, and the Word was God" (John 1:1). In this chapter and the following we will consider the New Testament evidence that brought the church to a settled conviction that Jesus Christ is God the Son, the same in substance, equal in power and glory with the Father.

In marketing, trademarks are used to distinguish the genuine from counterfeits. The Bible uses four trademarks to separate God from all pretenders: his divine names and titles, his divine attributes, the divine works he does, and the divine worship he receives. God reveals himself as the only true God. He states in the first commandment: "I am the LORD your God. You shall have no other gods beside me." With these words he distinguishes himself from all false gods; no one else is like him. The four trademarks apply exclusively to God. So when the New Testament writers attach these trademarks to Jesus, either directly or by implication, they are claiming deity for him.

The New Testament's Direct Evidence

The first trademark is the divine names. A name is important. At one time a man's name told a great deal about him. Johnson was the son of John. Smith was the village blacksmith. In the Bible, names are very important. Frequently, as in the case of Abraham and Isaac, God changed a man's name to say something about him.

The names of God, however, are always of the greatest importance. They are one of the primary ways we know him. Moreover, God is jealous of the glory of his names and titles. Therefore, it is significant that the New Testament writers, both directly and indirectly, ascribe divine names and titles to Jesus Christ.

God

In many places the New Testament writers unhesitatingly call Jesus divine names. They call him "God." As you look at some of these passages, keep in mind that in the Old Testament the word for *God*, "Elohim," is sometimes used of false gods; and at other times it is used of created beings. For example, Job 1:6 refers to angels as sons of God, and Psalm 82:16 addresses human rulers as gods. In fact, Jesus appeals to this psalm in a discussion with the Jews about his claims to deity (John 10:34, 35). In effect Jesus is saying, "Since God uses this title of mere men, why should you object to the use of it by me, the unique son of God?" In the few places where the name *Elohim* does not refer to the true God, however, the context makes it clear how we are to understand the term.

With this in view, I assert that New Testament writers call Jesus Christ "God" in the fullest sense of the term. The most familiar passage, of course, is John 1:1. Here John is describing Jesus Christ (John 1:14) and claims that Christ was with God and was God. In this verse John says two important things. First, he claims that Jesus Christ was and is God—totally, absolutely, equally God. Second, he teaches the plurality of the Godhead.

The group who call themselves Jehovah's Witnesses claim that the proper translation of the Greek in this place is "the word was 'a god'"—namely, a god less divine than the true God. They say this on the basis of the omission of the definite article *the* before the word *God*. True, the definite article *the* is not in the Greek. But as in English, the absence of the article does not mean that one must supply the indefinite article *a*. To say he is *God* is not to say he is *a* God!

The form of grammar used here is called a predicate nominative—two nouns joined by a form of the verb *to be*.

The first noun is the subject, the second is the predicate nominative—another noun designating the subject. In Greek the definite article is frequently omitted when the predicate nominative is a proper name. Words like *God* are treated as proper names. When we say "I love God," we don't have to add *the* to show that we mean the true God. Therefore to say he is God is to say he is *the* God. John claims Jesus is the true God.

The second truth John alludes to in this verse is the plurality that exists in the Godhead. Notice the strange phrase, "He was with God and he was God." How can someone be God and be with God? The answer is found in the doctrine of the Trinity as summarized by the Westminster Shorter Catechism: "There are three persons in the Godhead: the Father, the Son, and the Holy Ghost; and these three are one God, the same in substance, equal in power and glory" (Q/A 6). John 1:1 teaches us that God the Father and God the Son are one,

The background for this concept was established in the Old Testament revelation of the Angel of the Lord. We learned in Chapter 1 that the Angel of the Lord was one sent from the Lord. He was the messenger of the Lord, who *was* the Lord. One from the Lord who is the Lord—one alongside God who is God—a mystery solved by the fuller New Testament revelation of the person of Jesus Christ!

Another evidence that Jesus is God in the fullest sense of the term is found in Romans 9:5. Paul, describing the benefits of belonging to the Old Covenant people, says, "And from them is traced the human ancestry of Christ, who is God over all, forever praised!" The phrase beginning with *who* is a description of Christ. He is God over all. Paul, the archdefender of the exclusive divine rights of God, does not blush to claim that Jesus is the sovereign God.

Paul says the same thing in Titus 2:13: "We wait for the blessed hope—the glorious appearing of our great God and Savior, Jesus Christ." In this passage, Paul is exhorting us to godly living in light of the return of the Lord Jesus Christ, whom he describes as our great God and Savior. Is God the Father coming again? Is it *his* appearing for which we are looking? No! We are looking for the appearing of Christ Jesus. Paul calls him our great God and Savior. Again— absolutely, emphatically—he applies the name *God* to Christ Jesus. The writers of the New Testament consistently apply the trademark of *God* to Jesus Christ.

Lord

Another Old Testament title used exclusively of the true God is Lord. When God appeared to Moses on Mount Sinai, he revealed the full significance of this name. In response to Moses' question, "Whom shall I say sent me?" God said in Exodus 3:14, "Tell them that 'I am who I am' sent you."From this phrase God developed the personal name *Jehovah* or *Yahweh*, translated "Lord." The New Testament writers unhesitatingly ascribed this name to Jesus Christ.

When Thomas, a devout Jew, was faced with the reality of the resurrected Christ, he had no qualms in confessing, "My Lord and my God!" (John 20:28). In addition to calling Christ "God," Thomas called him "Lord." If Jesus were not God these words would have been blasphemous.

The Greek word for Lord is *kurios*. It is used in the Septuagint (the Greek translation of the Old Testament), to translate the word *Jehovah*. The New Testament writers were well aware of this when they applied the title to Jesus Christ. It is true that the title can suggest the idea of honor and reverence owed to a superior, but when used of Christ— particularly in the context of his risen glory—it implies that he is Jehovah. It refers to his present sovereignty and exalted power.

Paul uses *Lord* this way in his classic statement about Jesus Christ,

> Who, being in very nature God, did not consider equality with God something to be grasped, but made himself nothing, taking the very nature of a servant, being made in human likeness. And being found in appearance as a man, he humbled himself and became obedient to death—even death on a cross! Therefore God exalted him to the highest place and gave him the name that is above every name, that at the name of Jesus every knee should bow, in heaven and on earth and under the earth, and every tongue confess that Jesus Christ is Lord, to the glory of God the Father (Philippians 2:6–11).

In this passage the title *Lord* is given to Jesus Christ, the ascended God-man. This is an amazing concept! It means that the manifestation of the divine glory is not confined to Jesus' divine nature but extends to him as a person. He is frequently called the *Lord* Jesus Christ. In other words: Jesus of Nazareth, the anointed Savior, is Jehovah, the Lord. Trinitarians are the true Jehovah's witnesses, because Jehovah is a triune God! Jehovah is Father, Son, and Holy Spirit.

Son of God

A third title given to Jesus is *Son of God*. Just as the name *God* is used sometimes to refer to others than Jehovah God, so the phrase *sons of God* may be used of creatures. Moreover, sometimes it is used of Christ to express something besides his full deity. For example, he is called *the Son of God* with respect to his Messianic office.

The New Testament writers, however, use the phrase *Son of God* to teach his preexistent, equal relationship to God the Father. John writes of him in John 1:14 that he is the only begotten one (translated in the NIV "the one and only"). In John 3:16, this phrase is applied to Jesus as the unique Son of God.

In Romans 1:3 Paul uses the phrase *Son of God* to depict Christ's eternal sonship. He says that Jesus Christ, the focal point of the gospel, is God's Son who was born the son of David. Doesn't this language imply a preexistent relationship? He who is eternally God's Son became a man—he was born. But by his resurrection he is declared to be the Son of God in power, glory and honor (vs. 4).

Romans 8:3 and Galatians 4:4 use the same type of language. Paul says the Son of God was sent into the world in order to save us from our sins. Both of these verses teach that Jesus was the preexistent Son of God who became a man. The New Testament writers, by giving Jesus the names *God*, *Lord* and *Son of God*, teach that he is God.

The New Testament's Indirect Evidence

In addition to the direct claims, there are a number of indirect references to Christ's deity. The divinity of the Lord Jesus Christ is a golden thread woven through both Old and New Testaments. If we approach our Bibles in a careless, hit-or-miss fashion, we will miss a great deal of biblical truth. As a person immerses himself in his Bible, he develops a spiritual sixth sense. He accepts such truths as the Trinity and the sovereignty of God, not simply because of a verse here or there that teaches the truth, but because it is set forth in a multitude of ways throughout Scripture. The deity of the Lord Jesus Christ is just such a truth. It's not some obscure doctrine tucked away in a corner of the Bible—it's everywhere to be seen by one who is familiar with his Bible.

For example, a good musician may not need to see the composer's name to recognize who wrote a certain piece of classical music. If he knows the composer's work, he will recognize his style. In the same way, someone who knows art well doesn't have to see the artist's signature on a painting by a master—he will recognize the style. This is how it is with the deity of Jesus. It comes at us with all the force of the Scriptures and the power of the Holy Spirit; it inundates us, it overwhelms us. The Bible is full of indirect references to the deity of our Savior.

By indirect reference I mean the New Testament's application to Jesus Christ of Old Testament declarations about Jehovah. For example, in Hebrews 1:10–12 the writer quotes Psalm 102:25–27 to demonstrate the superiority of God the Son, our Savior, over the angels. A Jew reading Psalm 102 would recognize that these verses refer to the true God of the Bible. Nevertheless, the writer of Hebrews has no problem applying them to the Lord Jesus Christ. In other words, Jesus Christ is the God who is addressed in Psalm 102.

In Romans 14:11 and Philippians 2:10 Paul quotes Isaiah 45:23 and applies it to Jesus. However, in Isaiah 45 the prophet is speaking of Jehovah. The language is powerful. He says, "I am Jehovah, the incomparable God" (vs. 21). The New Testament, nevertheless, applies this claim to the Lord Jesus Christ.

A third example is John 12:41. As the Jews resist him, Jesus teaches that Isaiah had prophesied concerning their hard-heartedness and spiritual blindness. He quotes from Isaiah 6:10. John then adds by way of commentary that Isaiah said these things because he saw "his" glory. Whose glory? The glory of Jesus. But notice how Isaiah began this chapter: "In the year that King Uzziah died, I saw the Lord seated on a throne, high and exalted." Isaiah describes the holiness of

Jehovah; John applies it to the Lord Jesus Christ. Trinitarians are the true Jehovah's witnesses, because Jehovah is a triune God. Jehovah is Father, Son and Holy Spirit.

One other passage, Mark 1:2, 3, describes the ministry of John the Baptist as a fulfillment of Isaiah 40:3. Isaiah prophesied that the forerunner was to make ready the way of Jehovah. Mark applies this to John the Baptist, the forerunner of the Lord Jesus Christ.

What's in a name? Both by direct and indirect references, the New Testament ascribes divine names and titles to Jesus Christ. From his names we know he is God. Like Thomas, we must bow in humble, loving worship of Jesus, our God and Lord.

Review Questions

1. What are the four trademarks that distinguish the true God from false gods?

2. What three divine names do New Testament writers give to Jesus Christ?

3. What two things does John teach in John 1:1 about Jesus Christ and the Godhead?

4. List some of the New Testament references that apply the name *God* to Jesus Christ.

5. Where did the title *Lord* originate?

6. List some New Testament passages that give the title *Lord* to Jesus Christ.

7. List some of the indirect references to the deity of Jesus Christ.

Discussion Questions

1. Why is it important that a person believe in the full deity of the Lord Jesus Christ?

2. What do you think the Nicene Creed means when it says that the Lord Jesus Christ is "the Son of God, begotten of the Father as only begotten, that is, from the essence of the Father"?

3. Do a role play between a Christian and a Jehovah's Witness, using John 1:1 and indirect references to prove the deity of Jesus Christ.

4. The Larger Catechism, Q/A 109 says that the second commandment forbids "the making any representation of God, of all or of any of the three persons, either inwardly in our mind, or outwardly in any kind of image or likeness of any creature whatsoever." Should we then use pictures of the Lord Jesus Christ in educational materials?

3

THE IRREPRESSIBLE GLORY

The name *Cadillac* is the trademark for a quality luxury car. For many people, the name has become synonymous for top-of-the-line quality. The name suggests a certain glory.

There is also a glory that belongs to God alone. This glory cannot be repressed or restrained. It is clearly seen in four trademarks: his divine names, his divine attributes, the divine works he does, and the divine worship he alone has a right to receive.

In Chapter 2 we learned that Jesus Christ has the first trademark. The glorious names of God are given to him, so he must be God. In this chapter, we shall see that the other trademarks also belong to the Lord Jesus Christ. He has the divine attributes, he does divine works and he receives divine worship.

Divine Attributes

The Bible identifies a number of attributes or character-istics that God possesses in a manner unique to himself. These are called his incommunicable attributes. These are attributes that God does not communicate to or share with man. Among these attributes are eternity, immutability and omniscience. In the New Testament each of these incommunicable attributes is applied to the Lord Jesus Christ.

First, the Lord Jesus has the divine attribute of eternity.

In verse 1 of his gospel John states that Jesus, the Word, was God and was with God. Moreover, he states that the Word was eternal: "In the beginning was the Word" (1:1). This language, *In the beginning*, takes us back to Genesis 1:1 where we read, "In the beginning God created the heavens and the earth." Biblical writers use this phrase to point to the beginning of all things, a beginning before which only God existed. Thus, in John 1:1, the writer is telling us that Jesus Christ, the Word, is eternal.

When the Bible claims eternity for Jesus Christ, it is in light of the truth that eternity is an exclusive attribute of God. For example, Isaiah says, "This is what the Lord says— Israel's King and Redeemer, the LORD Almighty, I am the first and I am the last; apart from me there is no God" (Isaiah 44:6). Only God has no beginning and no end. Therefore, when the New Testament says that Jesus is eternal, it teaches that he is God.

The New Testament also teaches that Jesus has the attribute of immutability—the quality of unchangeableness. Like eternity, immutability is an attribute that belongs exclusively to the Lord God. God says of himself in Malachi 3:6, "I the LORD do not change. So you, O descendants of Jacob, are not destroyed." Hebrews 1:11, 12 tells us that, even though the creation will wear out, Jesus Christ remains the same. And in Hebrews 13:8 we read that Jesus Christ is the same yesterday, today and forever. The trademark of immutability demands that we assent to the deity of the Lord Jesus Christ.

One other incommunicable attribute ascribed to Jesus is omniscience. According to Psalm 139, the Lord God knows everything, even our thoughts and our motives. In his dedicatory prayer in 1 Kings 8:39, Solomon says to the Lord, "Then hear from heaven, your dwelling place. Forgive and act; deal with each man according to all he does, since you know his heart (for you alone know the hearts of all men)." God knows immediately, eternally and exhaustively.

The gospels give frequent examples of Jesus' exercising omniscience. Often he is depicted as knowing what his enemies were thinking. For example, Luke writes, "But Jesus knew what they were thinking and said to the man with the shriveled hand, 'Get up and stand in front of everyone'" (Luke 6:8). When Jesus claims equal knowledge with the Father, he is claiming omniscience. "All things have been committed to me by my Father. No one knows the Son except the Father, and no one knows the Father except the Son and those to whom the Son chooses to reveal him" (Matthew 11:27). He knows the Father in the same comprehensive manner the Father knows him. Jesus is no counterfeited copy; he is the all-knowing God.

Divine Work

The third divine trademark given to the Lord Jesus Christ is the ability to do works that are exclusively works of God. The Bible teaches that to God alone are ascribed the works of creation and providence; to God alone belongs the authority to forgive sin; to God alone is the execution of the judgment of men and angels.

The New Testament, however, ascribes each of these divine acts to the Lord Jesus Christ. We have already pointed out the relationship between Genesis 1:1 and John 1:1. Moses teaches in Genesis that God created all things. John the apostle tells us that Jesus Christ, the Word, is Creator: "Through him all things were made; without him nothing was made that has been made" (John 1:3).

As Creator, Jesus rules and sustains all things. For

example, the writer of Hebrews claims that Jesus Christ, who made all things, holds them together by his powerful word (Hebrews 1:3). Paul reinforces this truth while reflecting on the perfect glory of Jesus Christ:

> He is the image of the invisible God, the firstborn over all creation. For by him all things were created: things in heaven and on earth, visible and invisible, whether thrones or powers or rulers or authorities; all things were created by him and for him. He is before all things, and in him all things hold together (Colossians 1:15–17).

May we withhold divine honor from the one who has made and continues to sustain all things? The one who gives birth to the child is its mother. The one who gives birth to the creation is God.

Another example of Jesus' performing a divine work is found in Mark 2:1–12. Four men brought a paralytic friend to Jesus to be healed. Unable to get through the crowd, they lowered him through the roof of the house. In response to their faith, Jesus said to the paralytic, "Son, your sins are forgiven." Some of the Jewish leaders who were present were scandalized. "Why does this fellow talk like that? He is blaspheming! Who can forgive sins but God alone?"

The Jews were correct in their reasoning. They knew that the authority to forgive sins belongs to God alone. But their conclusion—"he is blaspheming"—was wrong. They failed to recognize that Jesus is the eternal Son of God and that he has God's authority to forgive. Therefore, Jesus challenged them,

> "Why are you thinking these things? Which is easier: to say to the paralytic, 'Your sins are forgiven,' or to say, 'Get up, take your mat and walk'? But that you may know that the Son of Man has authority on earth to forgive sins . . . ." He said to the

paralytic, "I tell you, get up, take your mat and go home." He got up, took his mat and walked out in full view of them all (Mark 2: 8–12).

In this passage, Jesus not only claims the authority to forgive sins, but also demonstrates that authority through the work of divine healing.

In addition to showing that Jesus has the power to create and uphold the world, and the authority to forgive sins, the New Testament also teaches Jesus has the right of divine judgment:

> Moreover, the Father judges no one, but has entrusted all judgment to the Son . . . . And he has given him authority to judge because he is the Son of Man (John 5:22, 27).

Jesus claims the authority both to raise the dead on the last day, and to exercise his rights as the supreme and sovereign judge over them.

The glory of Christ is indeed the irrepressible glory of God. The divine trademarks of names, attributes and works belong to Jesus Christ.

Divine Worship

The Bible teaches that it is a sin to worship anyone but the true God. The first commandment says, "You shall have no other gods before me" (Exodus 20:3), and throughout the Old Testament we are taught that divine worship and adoration are to be given to God alone. To worship anyone but God was a sin worthy of death. In Isaiah 42:8, God says, "I am the Lord; that is my name! I will not give my glory to another."

Jesus acknowledged that worship is to be given to God alone. When the devil showed Jesus all the kingdoms of the world and said, "If you worship me, these will be yours," Jesus rebuffed him: "Away from me, Satan! For it is written: 'Worship the Lord your God, and serve him only '" (Matthew 4:10).

Nevertheless, throughout the New Testament, we find the Lord Jesus Christ being given divine worship and accepting it. One of the clearest examples of this is in Revelation 4 and 5. Revelation 4 shows the Lord God, enthroned in heaven. The living creatures and elders worship him, saying:

> "Holy, holy, holy is the Lord God Almighty who was, and is, and who is to come. . . . You are worthy, our Lord and God, to receive glory and honor and power, for you created all things, and by your will they were created and have their being" (Revelation 4:8, 11).

In Revelation 5 John sees the Lord Jesus Christ as the Lamb who was slain. In this capacity, the living creatures and the elders worship him:

> "Worthy is the Lamb, who was slain, to receive power and wealth and wisdom and strength and honor and glory and praise! . . . To him who sits on the throne and to the Lamb be praise and honor and glory and power, for ever and ever!" (Revelation 5:12, 14).

The fact that Jesus is worshiped equally with God the Father is irrefutable evidence that he is truly God, the same in substance, equal in power and glory with the Father (SC, Q/A 6).

Jesus Aware of the Irrepressible Glory

Even though the New Testament writers give evidence that proves beyond any shadow of a doubt that the Lord Jesus Christ is God, some people suggest that this was only their opinion and that Jesus himself was not conscious of being God. After all, he never called himself God. But throughout the Gospels Jesus claims to be God's eternal Son. He claims to share equal knowledge and glory with the Father.

At twelve years of age, Jesus was already conscious of the special and unique relationship he had to God the Father. He had remained in Jerusalem to discuss the Scriptures with the scribes and teachers at the temple. When his parents found him and expressed their concern, he responded, "Why were you searching for me? . . . Didn't you know I had to be in my Father's house?" (Luke 2:49).

Later the Jews heard Jesus refer to God as his Father: "My Father is always at work to this very day, and I, too, am working" (John 5:17). They accused him of claiming equality with God. John continues, "For this reason the Jews tried all the harder to kill him; not only was he breaking the Sabbath, but he was even calling God his own Father, making himself equal with God" (5:18).

At the climactic confrontation at his trial, Jesus answered under oath that he is the eternal Son of God: "But I say to all of you: In the future you will see the Son of Man sitting at the right hand of the Mighty One and coming on the clouds of heaven" (Matthew 26:64). In response, the high priest tore his robe and said, "He has spoken blasphemy! Why do we need any more witnesses? Look, now you have heard the blasphemy. What do you think?" "He is worthy of death," they answered (Matthew 26:65, 66). Again, the Jews rightly understood that Jesus was claiming equality with God.

On another occasion Jesus told the Jews that Abraham had rejoiced to see his day. The Jews responded, "You are not yet fifty years old . . . and you have seen Abraham!" (John 8:57). Jesus responded, "I tell you the truth, . . . before Abraham was born, I am!" (vs. 58). They tried to stone him, thinking he committed the ultimate act of blasphemy by calling himself "I AM," the eternal name of God (Exodus 3:14).

These few examples demonstrate that Jesus considered himself to be God, possessing the irrepressible glory of the divine trademarks.

But some object, "If Jesus is indeed God, why does the New Testament depict him as inferior to the Father? For example, Jesus himself says, 'My food . . . is to do the will of him who sent me and to finish his work' (John 4:34). And in Matthew 26:39 he prays to the Father, 'If it is possible, may this cup be taken from me. Yet not as I will, but as you will.'"

The solution to this question is not difficult. The Son of God took on a human nature in order to become the servant of God and the servant of God's people (see Philippians 2:6–8). The writer to the Hebrews shows that Jesus had a body prepared for him so that he might perfectly fulfill the will of God and give himself as a sacrifice for sinners (10:4–9). When John the Baptist was hesitant to baptize him, Jesus said, "Let it be so now; it is proper for us to do this to fulfill all righteousness" (Matthew 3:15). As our divinely appointed Savior, Jesus was in submission to the Father; but this fact in no way casts doubt on his eternal deity.

The irrepressible glory of the divine attributes, work, and worship emphatically declare that *Jesus Christ is Jehovah God* (Figure 2). It is our duty to believe in him as the eternal Son of God and trust in him alone for our salvation. Apart from belief and trust in the divine Savior, there is no salvation. "If you confess with your mouth, 'Jesus is Lord,' and believe in your heart that God raised him from the dead, you will be saved. For it is with your heart that you believe and are justified, and it is with your mouth that you confess and are saved" (Romans 10: 9, 10).

DIVINE TRADEMARKS	THE LORD JESUS CHRIST
Names	
God	John 1:1; Rom. 9:5; Titus 2:13
Lord	John 20:28; Phil. 2:11
Son of God	Romans 1:3; Galations 4:4
Attributes	
Eternal	John 1:1
Immutable	Hebrews 1:11,12; 13:8
Omniscient	Luke 6:8; Matt.11:27
Work	
Creation	John 1:3
Providence	Hebrews 1:3; Col. 1:15–17
Pardon	Mark 2: 1–12
Judgment	John 5:22–27
Worship	Revelation 5:12,14

Figure 2

Review Questions

1. What are God's incommunicable attributes? List some of them.

2. What are some of the incommunicable attributes that are applied to the Lord Jesus Christ.

3. What divine works does the New Testament ascribes to Jesus Christ?

4. What do we learn from Revelation 5:12, 14 about Jesus Christ?

5. Was Jesus aware of his divinity? Give some examples to prove your answer.

6. How do you answer the person who says that the New Testament depicts Jesus in a role inferior to God the Father?

Discussion Questions

1. Is faith in the deity of Jesus Christ a blind acceptance of the teaching of the church, or assent to the clear teaching of Scripture?

2. How does the fourfold trademark bolster our confidence?

3. What comfort should Christians derive from the fact that Jesus Christ will be the Judge on the day of judgment?
4. Do another role play, using the arguments from this lesson to prove the deity of the Lord Jesus Christ.

4

MAN OR PHANTOM?

The early church father Polycarp, a disciple of the apostle John, tells of an incident where John abruptly left the public baths at Ephesus when he heard that a false teacher named Cerinthus had entered. John reportedly said, "Let us flee, lest the baths fall in while Cerinthus, the enemy of the truth, is within." Why did the gentle Apostle of Love react so vehemently against Cerinthus? Because Cerinthus denied the humanity of the Lord Jesus Christ.

We know that the Old Testament teaches that the Messiah was and is divine. He is the Root of David—David's Lord. Isaiah called him Mighty God, Everlasting Father, Prince of Peace, and Wonderful Counselor (9:6). But in order to be the Savior, this divine Person had to come and live among men and share in their suffering.

How could God come and live among men? If God showed himself to us as he is in his essential glory, such a revelation would destroy us. No man can see the essential glory of God and live (Exodus 33:20). Just as we cannot look fully into the sun, so we cannot look at God. He is an infinite, holy, consuming fire. His glory would destroy us in our sin. Thus, if God were to come as redeemer, he needed to reveal himself in a way that would not consume us.

To provide a solution to this dilemma, we must turn to the Old Testament teaching that the Messiah is the Branch of David (see Chapter 1). He is a man—a descendant of David.

His family tree goes back to Adam and Eve. The Messiah is true God and true man in one person.

To most of us this truth is old hat. However, not everyone in the history of the church has believed in the humanity of Jesus Christ. Just as some have attacked the deity of the Lord Jesus Christ, others have denied his humanity. Cerinthus was one of these heretics. He held to a variation of a doctrine called Docetism. The name comes from the Greek word which means "to seem" or "to appear." The Docetists were dualists. They believed that matter was evil and spirit was good. According to them, it was absurd to think that God would have taken on a human nature and that the material body of Jesus Christ would have been raised. They taught that Jesus of Nazareth only appeared to be a human being in a manner similar to God's assuming the appearance of a man in the Old Testament.

Cerinthus's teaching was a little different from other Docetists. He distinguished between the man, Jesus of Nazareth, and the Christ who he believed had descended in the form of a dove, enabling him to perform miracles and proclaim the Father. According to Cerinthus, the Christ departed before Jesus suffered and died. Thus it was only the human being who died. It is against this error that John supposedly recoiled in horror at the Ephesus baths. John writes:

> This is how you can recognize the Spirit of God: Every spirit that acknowledges that Jesus Christ has come in the flesh is from God, but every spirit that does not acknowledge Jesus is not from God. This is the spirit of the antichrist, which you have heard is coming and even now is already in the world (1 John 4:2, 3).

For the most part, Docetism is not an error currently being taught. However, even though we don't deny the doctrine of Christ's true humanity, there are those who seem to downplay it. We focus our attention on his deity and give little thought to his humanity. When we do this we don't have a whole Savior.

Becoming acquainted with the doctrine of the incarnation will help us understand the relationship between Christ's divine and human natures. The term *incarnation* means "in the flesh" and is used to summarize the great truth that God became a man. John boldly declares, "In the beginning was the Word, and the Word was with God, and the Word was God. . . . The Word became flesh and made his dwelling among us. We have seen his glory, the glory of the One and Only, who came from the Father, full of grace and truth" (John 1:1, 14). Wonder of wonders, the Word became flesh. The eternal Son of God actually took to himself a human nature!

New Testament Emphasis on Humanity

Just how important is the humanity of Jesus Christ? How important is oxygen to our lives? How important is a mediator to our salvation? Without Jesus' humanity we couldn't be saved!

We note this importance in the emphasis the New Testament writers place on Jesus' humanity. Sometimes, due to our necessary preoccupation with defending his deity, we miss the emphasis on his humanity—or perhaps find ourselves uncomfortable with it.

Consider Paul's great statement on Christ as mediator: "For there is one God and one mediator between God and men, the man Christ Jesus" (1 Timothy 2:5). Paul asserts that the only mediator between God and men is *the man*, Jesus Christ. Obviously, he is emphasizing the humanity of Jesus

Christ. He reveled in that truth.

We find the same emphasis in Paul's sermon to the Athenians: "For he has set a day when he will judge the world with justice by the man he has appointed. He has given proof of this to all men by raising him from the dead" (Acts 17:31). Again, note the emphasis: the judge of all men is a *man* who died and rose again from the dead.

Peter also emphasized the humanity of the Savior. In his sermon on the day of Pentecost he says, "Men of Israel, listen to this: Jesus of Nazareth was a *man* accredited by God to you by miracles, wonders and signs" (Acts 2:22; emphasis mine). Obviously apostolic preaching emphasized the humanity of the Lord Jesus Christ.

The Benefits of Jesus' Humanity

The New Testament writers emphasized the humanity of Jesus Christ because they considered him to be the last Adam. They drew analogies between the first Adam in the garden and the last Adam, Christ. Paul writes, "But Christ has indeed been raised from the dead, the firstfruits of those who have fallen asleep. For since death came through a man, the resurrection of the dead comes also through a man. For as in Adam all die, so in Christ all will be made alive" (1 Corinthians 15:20–22). The first Adam begot sin and death; the last Adam begot resurrection and life.

In Romans 5:12 Paul contrasts the first Adam and the last Adam and then says, "But the gift is not like the trespass. For if the many died by the trespass of the one man, how much more did God's grace and the gift that came by the grace of the one man, Jesus Christ, overflow to the many!" (Romans 5:15). Do you see what Paul is doing here? He lifts Christ up as the last Adam.

This comparison highlights the covenant structure of the Bible. The first Adam acted for the entire human race. He plunged the race into the despair, bondage and corruption of sin and brought all under the wrath of God. However, the fall of Adam in no way erased the demand of the covenant—perfect obedience—or the penalty of the covenant—death to covenantbreakers. If a person were to have life, if he were to be right with God, he would have to obey God perfectly. If he did not, he would have to pay the penalty for his disobedience: death. All are born under this twofold obligation.

That's why the apostles delighted in the humanity of Jesus Christ. As a true human being, he was the last Adam, the second covenant head. In this covenant capacity, he did for the elect race what Adam had failed to do: he obeyed the law perfectly, and he did this on behalf of his people. It took a man to meet the stipulations of covenant obedience. As Boaz had to be a kinsman in order to pay off Naomi's and Ruth's debts and restore the inheritance, so Jesus had to be our kinsman.

Moreover, it took a man to satisfy the penalty of the covenant. The soul that sins shall die. But Jesus, as the last Adam, could take the penalty of death upon himself. His humanity was the ground of his being the true substitute for sinners. This is why Paul exalts the humanity of the mediator "who gave himself as a ransom for all men" (1 Timothy 2:6).

For the same reason the writer of Hebrews insists that Jesus had a true human nature:

> Since the children have flesh and blood, he too shared in their humanity so that by his death he might destroy him who holds the power of death—that is, the devil—and free those who all their lives were held in slavery by their fear of death (Hebrews 2:14, 15).

If there were to be atonement for men's sins, a man had to accomplish it. In order to meet all the demands of God and to save us from our sins, the Savior had to be a man.

Another benefit of Jesus' humanity is his ability to understand and help us as our faithful priest. The Roman Catholic Church has a distant Jesus. With all their pictures and statues, they fail to grasp the significance of his humanity. Therefore, according to some Roman Catholic theologians, a person needs the intercession of the tender mother of Jesus and of the saints who have experienced human needs and weaknesses. They simply fail to understand the practical importance of Jesus' humanity. We need no man or woman to pave our way to Jesus. He is a man eminently qualified to help us.

> For this reason he had to be made like his brothers in every way, in order that he might become a merciful and faithful high priest in service to God, and that he might make atonement for the sins of the people. Because he himself suffered when he was tempted, he is able to help those who are being tempted. For we do not have a high priest who is unable to sympathize with our weaknesses, but we have one who has been tempted in every way, just as we are—yet without sin (Hebrews 2:17, 18; 4:15).

Because Jesus is a true human being, he really does understand. When we pour out our hearts to him in pain and sorrow, he sympathizes. And through the Holy Spirit, whom Jesus sends to be with us, he ministers to our real human needs. So it is of the most practical importance that the Lord Jesus Christ is absolutely human.

One other benefit of Christ's incarnation is his flesh-and-blood example of holiness. As the Word made flesh, he both reveals the perfection of God's attributes and personifies human holiness. He is what Adam would have become, had he not sinned. Thus, he is the pattern to which our lives must conform. Peter points this out:

> To this you were called, because Christ suffered for you, leaving you an example that you should follow in his steps. "He committed no sin, and no deceit was found in his mouth." When they hurled their insults at him, he did not retaliate; when he suffered, he made no threats. Instead, he entrusted himself to him who judges justly (1 Peter 2:21–23).

In his delight to do the will of God, in his careful obedience to the law of God, in his willingness to trust God in and for all things, Christ is the benchmark. He is the goal of our lives, as Paul writes: "I press on toward the goal to win the prize for which God has called me heavenward in Christ Jesus" (Philippians 3:14; see also Hebrews 12:2). He is the mold that shapes our humanity in its sanctification.

> And we know that in all things God works for the good of those who love him, who have called according to his purpose. For those God foreknew he also predestined to be conformed to the likeness of his Son, that he might be the firstborn among many brothers (Romans 8:28, 29).

Do you see now why John opposed Cerinthus so vehemently? Christ's humanity is absolutely necessary for our atonement, our help, our sanctification and our glorification. Apart from becoming a man Jesus could not save us. As the apostles reveled in his humanity, so ought we.

Jesus is everything that we need. We who are sinners need a Savior, a perfect man who can fulfill for us the demands of God and also atone for the sins we have committed. Jesus, the last Adam, rendered perfect obedience for us, and then offered his life as the sacrifice for our sins.

Furthermore, we need help. We are weak and frail; we

need one who can come alongside us to uphold us and strengthen us. Jesus of Nazareth, who is one of us, is more than sufficient for this need too.

Finally, we need an example. Often when children cry out, "I don't understand," their parents respond not by telling them again, but by showing them how to do their task. Christ says to us, "Look at me. Do you want to be holy? Follow my example. As I obeyed the law of God willingly, you obey. As I loved God and men, you love. As I humbled myself, you humble yourself." Jesus is everything you need. Do you know him as your Savior and helper and guide? Have you experienced the great truth of the Heidelberg Catechism,

> What is your only comfort in life and death? That I am not my own, but belong with body and soul, both in life and in death, to my faithful Saviour Jesus Christ. He has fully paid for all my sins with his precious blood, and has set me free from all the power of the devil. He also preserves me in such a way that without the will of my heavenly Father not a hair can fall from my head; indeed, all things must work together for my salvation. Therefore, by His Holy Spirit He also assures me of eternal life and makes me heartily willing and ready from now on to live for Him (Q/A 1).

Review Questions

1. What does the doctrine of the incarnation teach?

2. Why was Jesus' humanity important to the Apostles?

3. Why does Paul refer to Jesus as the last Adam?

4. What did Jesus fulfill as the last Adam?

5. What other benefits derived from his humanity?

Discussion Questions

1. Covenant theology teaches that God has always related to his people by a covenant. Discuss how Jesus related to the first covenant with Adam and what he did for us in that capacity.

2. Compare Leviticus 25:23–25 and Ruth 4:1–17 and discuss how Boaz's transaction is a picture of the work of the Lord Jesus Christ.

3. Many of us have not given much thought to the humanity of Jesus. Discuss some practical situations in which the reality of Jesus' humanity would be very helpful.

4. The children's Christmas hymn, "Away in the Manger," says of baby Jesus, "No crying he makes." If Jesus were really a man would he have cried as a baby when he was hungry or needed his diaper changed?

5

THE VIRGIN'S SON

In his book *Knowing God*, theologian J. I. Packer makes a startling statement: the great difficulty of the Christian faith is the incarnation!

> The real difficulty . . . lies, not in the Good Friday message of the atonement, nor in the Easter message of resurrection, but in the Christmas message of the incarnation. The really staggering Christian claim is that Jesus of Nazareth was God made man . . . God became man; the divine Son became a Jew; the Almighty appeared on earth as a helpless human baby, unable to do more than lie and stare and wriggle and make noises, needing to be fed and changed and taught to talk like any other child. And there was no illusion or deception in this: the babyhood of the Son of God was a reality. The more you think about it, the more staggering it gets. Nothing is so fantastic as this truth of the incarnation (pp. 45, 46).

Indeed, the incarnation is the great mystery of our faith. However, once you accept this mystery, it becomes the glue that holds everything else together. We have dealt with the importance and benefits of the incarnation. In this chapter we will consider Christ's conception in the womb of the virgin and the extent of his human nature.

Virgin Conception

The incarnation was accomplished through what is commonly called the virgin birth or the virgin conception. This great event is recorded by Luke in the opening chapters of his Gospel.

For four hundred years God had been silent. Then suddenly we find a bustling of divine activity, a chain reaction of revelations. In Luke 1:26–38 we read about the messenger that God sent to Mary. The angel informed Mary that she would conceive and bear a son (vs. 31). Mary was stunned: "How will this be . . . since I am a virgin?" (vs. 34). The angel replied that the conception would be a direct, creative act of God (vs. 35). The angel's message makes three things clear: (1) Mary is to have a son (vs. 31); (2) this son is to be conceived by the power of the Holy Spirit without a human father (vs. 35); and (3) the one born of Mary was to be the Son of God (vs. 35).

What an amazing revelation—God becomes a man through the vehicle of virgin conception! At the very moment of conception the second person of the Godhead enters into a personal union with the newly created human nature. The eternal Creator is born a baby; the sustainer of the universe has to be fed and have his diaper changed. Mystery of mysteries!

The paradox is captured in a hymn by William Walsham How:

> Who is this so weak and helpless,
> Child of lowly Hebrew maid,
> Rudely in a stable sheltered,
> Coldly in a manger laid?
> 'Tis the Lord of all creation,
> Who this wondrous path hath trod;
> He is God from everlasting,
> And to everlasting God.
> (*Trinity Hymnal*, 169)

The Scripture teaching about Jesus' miraculous conception and birth is summarized in the Westminster Shorter Catechism, Q/A 22:

> How did Christ, being the Son of God, become man? Christ, the Son of God, became man, by taking to himself a true body, and a reasonable soul, being conceived by the power of the Holy Ghost, in the womb of the virgin Mary, and born of her yet without sin.

The Extent of Jesus' Human Nature

A True Body

The writer of Hebrews insists that Jesus had a physical human body: "Since the children have flesh and blood, he too shared in their humanity so that by his death he might destroy him who holds the power of death—that is, the devil" (Hebrews 2:14). Jesus took a true human nature so that he could deliver flesh-and-blood people from the penalty of sin. Jesus of Nazareth was no phantom. He was a true man.

The New Testament description of Jesus' physical nature confirms this claim. Luke tells us that Jesus was subject to physical growth and development. Jesus was born as an infant and developed exactly like other babies: "The child grew and become strong" (Luke 2:40). Physically, there was no difference between his human body and ours. He had to go through the process of growth and development.

Furthermore, his human body was subject to physical needs and frailties. He could get very tired. In John 4:6, we find him weary from his journey. He was subject to physical appetites. Not only did he ask the Samaritan woman for a drink of water (John 4:7), but also on the cross he cried out, "I am thirsty" (John 19:28).

Of course, he suffered the greatest human frailty of all:

he died. John describes this amazing fact in one brief sentence: "With that, he bowed his head and gave up his spirit" (John 19:30). In Mark 15:44, 45, a Roman soldier verifies his death. The Savior died, and only someone possessing a human body could die.

A Reasonable Soul

In addition to a true body, Jesus had a reasonable soul. In other words, he had a soul just like yours and mine. Now the soul is the center of human life. It is the center of the spiritual aspect of life that enables us to know God and ourselves. It is the regulator of our emotions and affections. Jesus was conscious of possessing this faculty. In the Garden of Gethsemane he expresses soul anguish: "My soul is overwhelmed with sorrow" (Matthew 26:38).

Now if Jesus had a true human soul exactly like ours, he must have been subject to mental and spiritual development. Luke, in fact, describes such development: "And the child grew and became strong; he was filled with wisdom and the grace of God was upon him. . . . And Jesus grew in wisdom and stature, and in favor with God and men" (Luke 2:40, 52). This is not to suggest that he was ever unwise: he was perfect. However, the perfect wisdom of a five-year-old is different from that of a mature man. Jesus' wisdom was related to his mental, emotional, and spiritual development.

Perhaps you are asking, "If he was perfect, how could he progress?" Perfection in a human being does not rule out development. God's infinite perfection is unchangeable, but growth and development are part of human nature. A pediatrician tells the parents that their three-year-old boy is physically perfect. He means that the child is exactly what he ought to be at that age. However, if the boy is struck by some disorder that causes his legs not to grow, the legs which were perfect at three are imperfect at twelve.

Adam was perfect before the fall, but subject to change. If he had not sinned, he would have grown in his knowledge of and relationship with God. Thus, when Jesus was a child, his soul was just what the souls of Cain and Abel would have been as children had Adam not sinned. As a child, Jesus was physically and morally everything a child was meant to be, but he would not remain a child.

Jesus developed in his capacity to obey—that is suggested by these verses from Hebrews: "Although he was a son, he learned obedience from what he suffered and, once made perfect, he became the source of eternal salvation for all who obey him" (5:8, 9). We may look at Jesus' life as a series of tests. With each passed test he proceeded to a higher one until he was ready for the ultimate test of Gethsemane and Golgotha. Certainly, this is not to imply that he was ever disobedient. Simply stated, at twenty years of age Jesus was not ready for the ultimate test of the cross; God the Father was preparing his human nature for the ultimate test. His human soul grew from strength to strength through his testing, trials and sufferings, until he was ready to be the perfect sin offering.

A further evidence that Jesus possessed a human soul is the Bible's description of his emotional life. For example, he expresses anguish and turmoil (Matthew 26:28 and John 12:27). He weeps in grief and sorrow (Luke 19:41 and John 11:35). He is frequently moved by compassion (Matthew 14:14). Furthermore, the willful rebellion of the Jews filled him with righteous anger (Mark 3:5).

When we say that Jesus had a soul just like ours, we must make one great exception: he was sinless. By this we mean that he was born without original sin and in fact was incapable of sinning. This is what theologians call the impeccability of Christ. The writer of Hebrews declares that Jesus was without sin: "For we do not have a high priest who is unable to sympathize with our weaknesses, but we have one who has been tempted in every way, just as we are—yet was without sin" (4:15). The list of Jesus' attributes as our high priest (Hebrews 7:26) emphasizes this same truth: he is "one who is holy, blameless, pure, set apart from sinners."

Jesus himself was conscious of his sinlessness. When his enemies were looking for any excuse to find fault with him, he challenged them: "Can any of you prove me guilty of sin?" (John 8:46). On his last night with the apostles Jesus testified that he had no indwelling sin: "For the prince of this world is coming. He has no hold on me" (John 14:30).

Jesus did not commit sin. Moreover, he was incapable of sinning. Due to the perfect union of his two natures, Jesus could not sin. Of course, the question arises, "What does the Bible mean when it says that he is able to minister to us because he was tempted at every point as we are? How can he help us in temptation, if he couldn't sin?" He can help us because he was tempted with an intensity that far surpasses what you and I could endure. Therefore, he understands our wrestling with temptation and is equipped to sustain us. We are thoroughly sinful; Jesus is thoroughly sinless. Not only does this equip him to minister to us, it also qualifies him to be the perfect substitute on our behalf.

Thus we see that the Bible clearly teaches that Jesus was a true human being. Like you and me, he had a body and a soul. The reality of his human nature is summarized in his name, Jesus. The angel said to Joseph, "She will give birth to a son, and you are to give him the name Jesus, because he will save his people from their sins" (Matthew 1:21). Jesus is true man, the Branch of David, the Savior of sinful men.

The Necessity of the Virgin Birth

As you well know, many professing Christians deny the virgin birth and say it is unnecessary. But the Bible reveals a number of reasons why the virgin birth *is* necessary. First, it is a necessary fulfillment of Old Testament prophecy. When Joseph wanted to put Mary away and the angel assured him that she had conceived by the power of the Holy Spirit, Matthew concludes by quoting Isaiah 7:14: "All this took place to fulfill what the Lord had said through the prophet: 'The virgin will be with child and will give birth to a son, and they will call him Immanuel'—which means 'God with us'" (Matthew 1:22, 23). The Bible prophesied that the Messiah was to be born of a virgin. The supernatural circumstances of Jesus' birth confirm that he fulfills these messianic prophecies.

Second, it was necessary for the Messiah to be born of a virgin so he could be the Son of David and the Son of God at the same time. Matthew's genealogy shows that Jesus legally was the son of David through his stepfather, Joseph. By being the legal descendant of Joseph, he would have been in line to rule. But the promise in 2 Samuel 7:12 suggests that David's physical son would be the Messiah. This was accomplished through Mary, who was also a descendant of David. Luke, who begins his genealogy by saying that Jesus was supposedly the son of Joseph (3:23), gives Jesus' descent from David through Mary. This explains the difference between Luke's genealogy (3:23–38) and Matthew's (1:1–17). Jesus, then, was *legally* the heir to the throne through Joseph and *physically* a descendant of David through his mother, the virgin Mary. In this way the eternal Son of God became physically the son of David.

A third reason for the virgin conception is the necessity for the Savior to be sinless. No one born in the normal manner can escape the defilement of original sin (SC, Q/A 6). Although there is a mystery concerning the exact manner in which the guilt and corruption of Adam's first sin is passed to every individual, we know that it involves the covenantal headship of the physical father. It was for this reason that the men were circumcised in the Old Covenant. How was the Messiah to be a man and escape the corruption and guilt of sin? It was by means of the virgin conception. In this way, God supernaturally provided a sinless human nature. Therefore the virgin birth is not an unnecessary appendage to our faith, but a clear, biblical truth that must be maintained at all cost. The virgin birth is the way God became a man.

The incarnation and virgin birth are staggering mysteries. Let us marvel at the great wisdom of God, who knowing exactly what we needed, provided a Savior in the only way that would meet every need. Who can help but praise God for the virgin birth and incarnation!

Review Questions

1. What three things do we learn from the angel's announcement to Mary?

2. Review what the Bible says about Jesus' physical characteristics.

3. Review what the Bible says about Jesus' spiritual/emotional characteristics?

4. What does the doctrine of the impeccability of Christ teach?

5. How can Jesus be tempted as we are, if he was incapable of sinning?

6. Give three reasons why the virgin conception is important and necessary.

Discussion Questions

1. Do you agree with Packer's assessment of the incarnation? Why is this so staggering?

2. Do you think a person can be a Christian and not accept the virgin birth?

3. Why is the doctrine of impeccability important?

4. What does the angel's announcement and the fact of the virgin conception teach us about the human life of a fetus at the moment of conception?

6

MYSTERIOUS UNION

About six hundred bishops from throughout Christendom gathered on the coast of the Bosporus at the city of Chalcedon in A.D. 451 for the largest church council yet to be assembled. What brought such an august body together? A controversy raging over the relationship of the divine and human natures of the Lord Jesus Christ.

We have examined two marvelous truths, the deity of the Lord Jesus and his full humanity. Our Savior is Lord—Jehovah—and he is Jesus—the man; he is both the root and branch of David. Now we must consider the relationship of the two natures joined together in the one person. Although the root and branch are different they make up one tree.

The teaching that two natures are joined together in the one person, Jesus Christ, is as mysterious as the doctrine of the Trinity. Our minds fail under the weight of the truth that the one person Jesus Christ possessed two distinct natures. The matter is further complicated by the fact that, as with the doctrine of the Trinity, the Bible does not give us a succinct, systematic statement. We must take all that the Scripture says about the nature of the God-man and put the information together in the most systematic form possible. Historically, this was done at the Council of Chalcedon.

This council was called to deal with the issues that had grown out of the Arian controversy. You remember Arius denied that Jesus was the same in substance, equal in power and glory with the Father. According to Arius, Jesus was a created, lesser god. This issue was settled at the Council of Nicea, where the church reaffirmed its commitment to the full eternal deity of the second person of the Godhead.

Having settled the issue of Christ's deity, the church needed to work out the problem of the relation of his deity to his humanity. The church refuted the doctrine of the Docetists and confessed the full humanity of Jesus as well as his deity. But how did the two natures come together? How did they relate? Simply confessing, "I believe that Jesus is God and man," did not resolve the differences. We can illustrate the problem with a political analogy. Both Republicans and Democrats believe that there ought to be local and federal government. But sharp controversy arises over the relation of the one to the other. So it was in the early church. The issue was finally settled at the Council of Chalcedon. Although they couldn't solve the mystery, the delegates agreed that Jesus was God *and* man, and they made a series of statements that since then have been the orthodox confession of the church. Take a moment to read the creed in Appendix B.

The essence of this creed is found in what the Westminster Confession of Faith says of the God-man:

> The Son of God . . . did . . . take upon him man's nature . . . . So that two whole, perfect, and distinct natures, the Godhead and the manhood, were inseparably joined together in one person, without conversion, composition, or confusion. Which person is very God, and very man, yet one Christ, the only Mediator between God and man (WCF, 8.2).

The two essential elements of this definition are summarized in the Shorter Catechism, Q/A 21:

> Who is the Redeemer of God's elect? The only Redeemer of God's elect is the Lord Jesus Christ, who, being the eternal Son

of God, became man, and so was, and continueth to be, God and man in two distinct natures, and one person, forever.

Jesus Christ is one person with two distinct natures.

One Person

The first thing affirmed in the Shorter Catechism, Q/A 21 is that Jesus Christ the God-man is one person. By *person* we mean that he has characteristics that make him a specific individual with his own personality. A person is the individualized expression of human nature with a distinct personality and set of gifts and abilities. All of us are human beings, but each of us is a person distinct from others.

Thus, we maintain that Jesus has a fully divine nature—in other words, all the qualities that make God *God*. He also has a true, fully human nature—all the qualities that make man *man*. But at the same time, we also insist that he has one distinct personality. He does not have two personalities. He's not schizophrenic, sometimes slipping into his human personality, unaware of the divine, while at other times assuming the divine, unaware of the human. He is one person and has one personality.

The unifying aspect of his personality is the second person of the Godhead. The second person of the Godhead, the eternal *Logos*, entered into personal union with the human nature created from the genetic structure of Mary. Just as our material body has never existed apart from its personal union with our soul, so Jesus' human nature was immediately brought into union with the divine person. His human nature never had a separate personality of its own, but from its origin was governed by the personality of the second person of the Godhead.

Several reasons lead us to conclude that the God-man was one person. First, there is no evidence in the Scriptures of a dual personality ascribed to the Lord Jesus Christ. Although the Bible clearly speaks of the Father, Son and Holy Spirit as three distinct persons, it never speaks of the God-man in this way. The Bible assigns individuality to each of the three members of the Godhead. For example, at the baptism of Jesus all three persons interacted simultaneously. God the Spirit, in the form of a dove, descended on God the Son while God the Father spoke from heaven (Matthew 3:16, 17).

This type of interaction is not found in Jesus Christ. God the Son does not speak to the man, Jesus. Rather, Jesus always speaks of himself as *I, my* or *me*. Nor do we find others speaking to him in any way but as to one person. Queen Elizabeth II is one person who is queen, wife and mother. As queen she doesn't speak to the mother or as wife to the queen. So in Jesus the divine nature does not speak to the human.

Someone might offer John 3:10, 11 as an exception:

"You are Israel's teacher," said Jesus, "and do you not understand these things? I tell you the truth, *we* speak of what *we* know, and *we* testify to what *we* have seen, but still you people do not accept *our* testimony. I have spoken to you of earthly things and you do not believe; how then will you believe if I speak of heavenly things?" (emphasis mine).

In this passage Jesus refers to himself in the plural. But notice how this reference is surrounded by personal singular references: "I tell you the truth," and afterwards, "If I speak." By the use of *we*, Jesus is referring to the testimony of others in addition to his own preaching and teaching. It is clear from the context that when he refers to himself he speaks singularly.

Second, the Bible teaches the unity of the person Jesus by referring to his two natures under one personal name or title. The title "Queen Elizabeth" describes the one person who is queen, wife and mother. Paul uses the title "Jesus Christ" *our Lord* in referring to the Savior, and describes him as the son of David according to the flesh, who was declared to be the eternal Son of God by his resurrection from the dead (see Romans 1:3, 4). Note that although he is described in terms of his two natures, the seed of David and the Son of God, Jesus is identified as one person under the title "Jesus Christ our Lord."

Third, the union of the two natures in the one person is taught by passages that describe the attributes of the one nature to the person while calling him by a title derived from the other nature. When we say "Queen Elizabeth is a good wife," we are describing her domestic character while using her royal title. Similarly, divine attributes and actions are ascribed to Jesus when he is called by a human title. For example, Isaiah refers to him as the son of David and at the same time says he is mighty God and everlasting Father (9:6, 7). On the other hand, human attributes are used to describe him when he is designated by a divine title. Paul refers to him as God who purchased the church with his blood (Acts 20:28).

These three lines of argument demonstrate that the Bible teaches that Jesus had one distinct personality.

Two Natures

As soon as we declare that Jesus Christ is one person, however, we are faced with the problem of the interrelation of the two natures within the one person. The second thing that the Shorter Catechism, Q/A 21 teaches is that the person Jesus Christ, the God-man, possesses two distinct natures.

When we speak of the nature of something, we mean the particular characteristics that make it what it is. For example, the nature of water is that it is a liquid consisting of two parts hydrogen to one part oxygen. Therefore the nature of something is defined by those qualities that make it what it is. The general definition of human nature is a physical body with a reasonable soul. The general definition of divine nature is a spiritual being who is infinite, eternal and unchangeable. In the one person, Jesus Christ, a truly human nature and a truly divine nature are inseparably united. But how do they interrelate? The church developed a right understanding of this doctrine as it struggled with a number of heresies.

The first heresy was called Appolinarianism. Appolinarius taught that the divine reason in Christ, the Logos, took the place of the human mind or reason which distinguished men from animals. Therefore, in Jesus Christ the human nature consisted only of material and animal part, and the divine nature took the place of the mind or spirit. This teaching was condemned by the Council of Constantinople in A.D. 381.

Another error was Nestorianism. This error was named after Nestorius, who taught that Christ was two separate persons. Jesus was a morally perfect man, who was upheld and strengthened by the divine reason or Logos. The more the human being obeyed, the more of the divine person was given to him, until, as a final reward at his ascension, he was given a full communication of the Godhead. The Council of Ephesus condemned this heresy in A.D. 431.

A third error was Eutychianism. Eutychius taught that there was only one nature (this error was also called Monophysitism). He maintained that Jesus Christ possessed only a divine nature which was clothed in humanity. The Council of Chalcedon condemned Eutychianism in A.D. 451.

A fourth error was Monothelitism. In response to the Council of Chalcedon, the advocates of this view held that Jesus was one person with two natures, but with only one divine will. This error was condemned by the Council of Constantinople in A.D. 681.

In contrast to all these errors, the church confesses the mysterious union. The language of the Westminster Confession of Faith, 8.2 gives the doctrinal summary of the conclusion of Chalcedon. It says Jesus had two distinct natures "inseparably joined together in one person, without conversion, composition, or confusion." This language tells us three things that are *not* true about the union. "Without conversion" means that there was no transformation of the two natures in the one person. The human nature is not converted into divine or vice versa in the way that medieval alchemists sought to turn base metals into gold. No, Jesus maintained two distinct natures.

"Without composition" means that the one person is not an alloy. An alloy is a substance that is formed from the mixture of two or more metals. For example, bronze is an alloy of copper and tin. In Christ, each nature retains its own properties unchanged. The human nature is finite, at times ignorant, susceptible to weakness, pain, human emotions, and death. The divine nature is infinite, eternal, omniscient, omnipotent, and subject to no change whatsoever. They did not combine to form a third nature.

"Without confusion" means that he is not part one thing and part another like a penny which is copper-plated zinc—neither 100 percent copper nor 100 percent zinc. He is not one-third man and two-thirds divine. Nor are divine attributes transferred to his human nature.

The Westminster Confession also says that Jesus possesses "two whole, perfect, and distinct natures . . . inseparably joined together in one person." The best way to understand this inseparable union is by the analogy of a human being who possesses a soul and a body. All of us know that we are people, but we know further that our human nature consists of these two distinct elements. Furthermore, although the two elements act together in a union, they can be separated. At death, the body is separated from the soul, and the soul goes to its eternal reward.

Because soul and body are united, a person speaks using singular pronouns, regardless of whether what is said reflects soul, or body, or the whole person. For example, if I stub my toe, I can say either, "My toe hurts," or "I hurt." When Jesus prayed in the Garden of Gethsemane, he said, "My soul is overwhelmed with sorrow." He could equally well have said, "I am overwhelmed with sorrow."

In the same manner, our Savior sometimes spoke according to his human nature. He referred to his fatigue, his hunger, his grief and his anger. At other times, he spoke according to his divine nature, as the authoritative Son of God, the eternal Jehovah. But he did not usually distinguish between the natures by saying, "Now speaking as a man, I am hungry" or, "Now speaking as God, I have the authority to raise the dead." Rather he says, "I am hungry," or he says, "I forgive your sins." As he is the one person possessing inseparably the two natures, whatever either nature does, the person does.

This doctrine of the one person's possessing two distinct natures is called the hypostatical or personal union. The mystery of this union in no way detracts from its importance. In fact, throughout the centuries the church has emphasized this doctrine because of its importance to the mediatorial work of the Lord Jesus Christ.

If you think for a moment, you will realize why this doctrine is important. We insist that the Savior is one person with two distinct natures in order to establish the truth that the Mediator, the Lord Jesus Christ, was one person acting on behalf of the people given to him and that everything done by him was both human and divine.

On the one hand, the Mediator, the Savior of sinners, had to be a man. Men sinned, and so their substitute must be a man. He must give human obedience, and he must suffer human punishment. On the other hand, if he were *merely* a man, it would be impossible for him to satisfy an eternal debt. He could not, in a few short hours on the cross, satisfy the infinite, eternal debt of sin. But because he is God, his divine nature gave eternal efficacy to everything he did. Therefore it is important that we maintain that he is one person, possessing two distinct natures, human and divine. All that the human nature did was done by the one person; all that the divine nature did was done by the one person.

Furthermore, we can delight in the knowledge that our Savior continues to this day and through all eternity to be the eternal God-man—the one person. In a most remarkable manner, having joined our nature to his, he has exalted our nature in the unity of his person and bestowed upon it the glory that is rightfully his as divine. Therefore, as the God-man he is to be worshiped as the eternal Son of God. Moreover, the exaltation of his human nature is the guarantee to us that our human natures shall one day be lifted up in glory. He wears our human nature as the pledge that one day we shall be with him.

Review Questions

1. What two great truths about the Lord Jesus Christ are taught in the Shorter Catechism, Q/A 21?

2. What do we mean when we say that Jesus Christ is one person?

3. Give the reasons why we believe the Bible teaches that Jesus Christ is one person.

4. What does it mean that Jesus has two natures?

5. What does the Westminster Confession of Faith, 8:2 tell us about the union of the two natures and the one person?

6. List and describe the errors in the early church over the union of the natures in the one person.

7. What do we call this doctrine? Why is it important to insist on this doctrine?

Discussion Questions

1. The church developed the orthodox doctrine of the Person of the Lord Jesus Christ as it had to deal with error. What do you think is the role of the church in understanding the Bible? How important is a knowledge of church history to a twentieth-century Christian?

2. Many cults offer divinity to those who accept their teaching. On the basis of the perfect work of Jesus Christ the God-man, what is the Christian's hope in eternity?

7

CHRIST THE WORD

"A penny for your thoughts," we frequently say when our companion is quiet and reflective. Why? Because only by words do we know what a person is thinking. The apostle John introduces us to the Savior by the title *the Word* (John 1:1). This title suggests that Jesus of Nazareth, the eternal Son of God who became man, is the spokesman for God. He shows and tells who God is and what God thinks. In other words, he is God's prophet.

As our Savior, Christ executes or performs the offices of a prophet, of a priest and of a king (SC, Q/A 23). These three offices in the Old Testament were preparatory to and revelatory of the work of the Messiah. Adam, having been created with knowledge, righteousness and holiness, was to serve God as a prophet, priest and king. When Adam sinned and lost his knowledge, righteousness and holiness, he of course compromised his ability to function properly in those offices. He who should have been God's prophet became the spokesman of Satan. He who should have been God's priest served Satan. He who should have been God's king became a slave of Satan. Thus the Savior would have to perform the offices of prophet, priest and king as part of his work in restoring to us knowledge, righteousness and holiness.

The Office of Prophet

Today, when we hear the term *prophet*, what most frequently comes to mind? A person who predicts the future.

But prediction was a secondary aspect of the biblical prophetic office. The English word *prophet* means "to set forth" or "to speak forth." A prophet spoke to men on God's behalf, declaring to them the Word of God. The concept of prophet is illustrated in the relationship of Moses and Aaron. When Moses complained that he was not a public speaker, God said:

> "You shall speak to him [Aaron] and put words in his mouth; I will help both of you speak and will teach you what to do. He will speak to the people for you, and it will be as if he were your mouth and as if you were God to him" (Exodus 4:15, 16).

Aaron was to be Moses' prophet to Pharaoh. God would give his words through Moses to Aaron, who would be the spokesman. God stood behind Moses and guaranteed the veracity of those words:

> Then the Lord said to Moses, "See, I have made you like God to Pharaoh, and your brother Aaron will be your prophet. You are to say everything I command you, and your brother Aaron is to tell Pharaoh to let the Israelites go out of his country" (Exodus 7:1, 2).

In respect to Pharaoh, Moses represented God and Aaron was his prophet or his mouthpiece.

Therefore the great task of a prophet was to deliver God's words. In the Old Testament, this office was essential to the well-being of the covenant people. The three aspects this office are set out in Deuteronomy 18:15–22.

First, a true prophet was one who had been called by God. "The Lord your God will raise up for you a prophet like me" (vs. 15; see also vs. 18).

Second, a true prophet was one who spoke by God's authority. "I will put my words in his mouth, and he will tell them everything I command him. If anyone does not listen to my words that the prophet speaks in my name, I myself will call him to account" (vss. 18, 19). When the prophet delivered a message from God, it was as if God himself were standing there audibly speaking.

Third, the true prophet was identified by the accuracy of his message. When the people asked, "How can we know if a man is a true prophet or a false prophet?" the answer was simple: "See if everything he predicts comes to pass." In his Word God gave two tests of a prophet. One was that his message was to be consistent with what had already been revealed by God (Deuteronomy 13:1–5). The second was that all his predictions must come to pass (Deuteronomy 18:21, 22; cf. 1 Kings 22:27, 28).

The work of the Old Testament prophet pictures the work of the Messiah. The Deuteronomy passage not only speaks generically of all true prophets; according to Acts 3:20–23, it also refers specifically to the Messiah, the prophet par excellence.

How, then, does Christ fulfill the office of prophet? "Christ executeth the office of a prophet, in revealing to us, by his Word and Spirit, the will of God for our salvation" (SC, Q/A 24). He was the preincarnate prophet of the Old Covenant. He was the incarnate prophet during his earthly ministry. He is the exalted prophet at the present time.

The Preincarnate Prophet

Did you know that Jesus Christ, as the eternal Son of God, has always functioned in the capacity of spokesman for the Godhead? This is why John calls him "the Word" in John 1:14 and why in Proverbs 8 he is alluded to as "the Wisdom of God." The Son of God has always been the spokesman for the Godhead.

He was God's spokesman at creation. When God said, "Let there be . . ." God the Son was the one speaking. This is why John tells us that all things were made by the Word (John 1:1–3; cf. Colossians 1:16; Hebrews 1:2). God who spoke all things into existence was God the Son. Creation is the first example of his activity as the Word of God.

But there are other examples. In fact, every Old Testament manifestation and revelation of the Godhead was through God the Son. We've already noted in Chapter 1 that the Angel of the Lord was the second person of the Godhead. In any of the theophanies (the physical, symbolic appearances of God), it is God the Son who reveals God to the people. For example, in the theophany of the pillar of cloud and fire, the Angel of God, the second person of the Godhead, is the one in the cloud revealing the presence of God. We read that when the Angel of the Lord moved, the cloud moved (Exodus 14:19). Thus, theophanic revelations were given by God the Son.

Visual revelations of Jehovah in human form were also mediated through God the Son. Of course, the greatest example is Isaiah's vision. "I saw the Lord seated on a throne, high and exalted" (Isaiah 6:1). The apostle John tells us Isaiah wrote this because he saw Jesus' glory (John 12:41). When God revealed himself in visions and theophanies, it was always through God the Son. He is the spokesman, the revealer of the Godhead.

Furthermore, note that when God revealed himself through the Old Testament prophets, it was God the Son who spoke through the prophets. Peter makes this clear:

Concerning this salvation, the prophets, who spoke of the

grace that was to come to you, searched intently and with the greatest care, trying to find out the time and circumstances to which the Spirit of Christ in them was pointing when he predicted the sufferings of Christ and the glories that would follow (1 Peter 1:10, 11).

Who was speaking through the Old Testament prophets? *The Spirit of Christ*. God the Son was speaking by the Holy Spirit through the Old Testament prophets. God the Son was the revealer of the Godhead in the Old Testament.

The Incarnate Prophet

The incarnation itself was the greatest prophetic work of the Son of God, for the incarnate Christ is the greatest revelation of God. He is the true theophany. John says, "The Word became flesh and made his dwelling among us. We have seen his glory, the glory of the One and Only, who came from the Father, full of grace and truth" (John 1:14). John adds in verse 18, "No one has ever seen God, but God the One and Only, who is at the Father's side, has made him known." To see Jesus, the Word, was to see the glory of God; to see Jesus, God the Son, was to see God himself. When the disciples asked to see the Father, Jesus said to Philip, "Don't you know me, Philip, even after I have been among you such a long time? Anyone who has seen me has seen the Father. How can you say, 'Show us the Father'?" (John 14:9). The God-man Jesus Christ is the perfect revelation of God. He is God in the flesh (Hebrews 1:1–3). The person Jesus Christ is the Word of God—God living in the midst of his people. He is the ultimate revelation of God.

Jesus revealed God through his works as well as through his person. When Jesus told his enemies that he was doing the Father's works, the Jews recognized that he was claiming equality with the Father. The work of the God-man was the

Father's work, and since it was the Father's work, it was the revelation of the Father (John 5:17–20).

In the revelation of Jesus, words and action are closely related. Luke says, "All the people were amazed and said to each other, 'What is this teaching? With authority and power he gives orders to evil spirits and they come out!'" (Luke 4:36). The teaching to which they referred was his miracles. They recognized the authority of revelation in the actions performed by Jesus. The two disciples on the road to Emmaus made a similar observation. Referring to Jesus, they said, "He was a prophet, powerful in word and deed before God and all the people" (Luke 24:19).

The third way that Jesus exercised the office of prophet while on earth was by his teaching. Jesus claimed to be teaching God's message. He said that he communicated what he had heard from the Father. "He who does not love me will not obey my teaching. These words you hear are not my own; they belong to the Father who sent me" (John 14:24). His teaching was directly from God. His words were every bit as authoritative as the Old Testament. He fully revealed God's mind to the people.

Because he reveals God perfectly, Jesus is the perfect interpreter of the Old Testament. He who had spoken through the prophets opened the disciples' understanding to the truth of the Old Testament.

> And beginning with Moses and all the Prophets, he explained to them what was said in all the Scriptures concerning himself. . . . He said to them, "This is what I told you while I was still with you: Everything must be fulfilled that is written about me in the Law of Moses, the Prophets and the Psalms." Then he opened their minds so they could understand the Scriptures. (Luke 24:27, 44, 45).

From the entire Old Testament Scriptures he taught them about himself. As God's prophet, he rightly interpreted the Old Testament.

Furthermore, as God's prophet he spoke with great authority. Notice how the people responded to his sermon in Matthew 7:28, 29. "When Jesus had finished saying these things, the crowds were amazed at his teaching, because he taught as one who had authority, and not as their teachers of the law." As the ultimate spokesman of God, he set forth God's message with God's authority. He came as the spokesman to bring God's message; he had the correct interpretation of the Old Testament. He had God's revelation, and he delivered that revelation and its interpretation with absolute authority. By his person, work and words, Jesus was God's prophet during his earthly ministry. Thus the writer of Hebrews says, "In the past . . . . by his his powerful word" (Hebrews 1:1–3).

The Exalted Prophet

If Jesus is God's ultimate prophet, how do we account for the New Testament, which was written after his ministry on earth? The answer is found in the truth that Jesus exercises his office as prophet not only in his preincarnate state and during his ministry on earth, but also from his exalted throne. He continues his prophetic work right now.

Jesus the prophet gave his final revelation through his apostles. Jesus promised his disciples, "The Counselor, the Holy Spirit, whom the Father will send in my name, will teach you all things and will remind you of everything I have said to you" (John 14:26). He also said,

> "But when he, the Spirit of truth, comes, he will guide you into all truth. He will not speak on his own; he will speak only what

he hears, and he will tell you what is yet to come. He will bring glory to me by taking from what is mine and making it known to you. All that belongs to the Father is mine. That is why I said the Spirit will take from what is mine and make it known to you" (John 16:13–15).

Christ promised that the Spirit would take his words and give them to the apostles.

The Spirit accomplished this in three ways. In the first place, the Spirit enabled the apostles to remember accurately and record faithfully, without error, everything they were to write about Jesus' ministry and message. Second, the Spirit enabled the apostles to interpret the Old Testament in light of what Jesus said and did. Third, the Spirit of Christ worked through the apostles and brought them to understand the implications and consequences of what Jesus said and did.

Everything in the New Testament falls under one of these three categories: It is the record either of (1) what Jesus said and did, (2) how Jesus' words and actions fulfill and interpret the Old Testament, or (3) how his words and actions form what we believe and how we live. Christ, in his prophetic office, gave the message by his Spirit to his apostles. That is why we claim that the Scriptures are the final revelation of God. Every book of the Bible in both the Old and the New Testaments is given by inspiration of God and is Scripture (2 Timothy 3:16, 17).

The Scriptures are Christ's words, and he speaks to us through all of them. It is erroneous to emphasize Jesus's words with red letters as some versions of the Bible do. The words spoken by Jesus during his earthly ministry are no more important than those he spoke throughout Scripture through his prophets and apostles.

One other way Christ continues to exercise his prophetic function is by opening our minds to understand and remember his words. This is his ongoing teaching function. He gives us the Holy Spirit, who makes the Scriptures clear to us. When you and I take our Bibles and prayerfully read them, Christ our prophet speaks to us by his Holy Spirit, through the Scriptures. And when we hear the Word of God faithfully and accurately preached, Christ the Word of God, the true prophet, speaks to us by his Holy Spirit.

He is our prophet. Therefore, you and I are responsible to pay careful attention to the word of God, to seek out and listen to the voice of Christ in the Scriptures. "If anyone does not listen to my words that the prophet speaks in my name, I myself will call him to account" (Deuteronomy 18:19).

We are not to be the judges of the Scriptures. That is, we are not to come to the Bible as judges of its authority. Nor are we to be sermon-tasters, evaluating sermons by style. Just as we subject ourselves to the Scriptures, so we subject ourselves to the preaching of the Word. We hear, "Thus saith the Lord." We are to listen to the voice of Christ as he speaks to us. We are to test what we hear by the Scriptures, but we may not reject a sermon just because we don't like it or don't care for the way it is packaged. Furthermore, we must believe all the doctrines of the Scriptures, and seek to practice all the commandments and laws of Scripture as they apply to us.

What a wonderful privilege is ours! When we study our Bibles, we have in effect a personal discipling conference with the Lord Jesus Christ. He sits with us by his Spirit and speaks to us from his Word in order to make us like himself. That is why it is such a great privilege to have the Word of God. We need to be faithful in our reading and studying of the Scriptures and in our attendance upon the preaching of God's Word.

Review Questions

1. What were the chief functions of the Old Testament prophet?

2. How did the preincarnate Christ exercise the office of prophet?

3. How did Jesus Christ perform the office of prophet during his ministry on the earth?

4. How was Christ's office of prophet fulfilled in the writing of the New Testament?

5. How does the Lord Jesus Christ exercise his office of prophet today?

6. What is to be our response to Jesus Christ as prophet who speaks to us through the Bible?

Discussion Questions

1. Are Jesus' words in the Gospels more authoritative than Paul's letters? Defend your answer.

2. What wrong impression may one derive from red-letter editions of the New Testament?

3. Why is preaching so important? How then should we listen to preaching?

4. If Jesus is the final revelation, how should we regard claims today of continuing revelation?

8

THE GREAT HIGH PRIEST

What a day! Clothed in beautiful linen garments, the high priest entered the holiest place of God's temple in order to make atonement for the sins of the people. He wore bells on the hem of his garment so that the people could hear him move about and know that God had accepted his offering. This was an awesome day. It was Yom Kippur, the Day of Atonement, the high point of Jewish worship—and the work of the high priest on this great day graphically pictures the work of the Lord Jesus Christ.

We have already learned that, as prophet, Jesus speaks to us on behalf of God. In this chapter we shall see that, as priest, Christ enables us to come to God.

The Necessity of a Priest

From the moment of the fall, mankind has been disqualified from coming to God. God is a holy, consuming fire. He declared that the soul that sins shall die. For this reason, God instituted sacrifices. Sin must be punished if God is to be reconciled to the sinner.

From the first, God appointed certain men as priests to make these sacrifices for themselves and others. We cannot come into God's presence without a priest. Earthly priests are evidence of the need we all have for an intercessor, a mediator between us and God.

Up to the time when the children of Israel assembled at Mount Sinai, the head of each family functioned as priest. For example, both Abel and Cain were responsible for bringing their sacrifices to God (Genesis 4:3). We note the same thing in connection with Noah (Genesis 8:20) and the patriarchs Abraham, Isaac, and Jacob (Genesis 12:7; 27:25; 35:6, 7).

In addition to the family priests, specific individuals functioned as priests on a larger scale. The most famous one is Melchizedek (Genesis 14). When Abraham returned from defeating the kings, "Melchizedek king of Salem brought out bread and wine. He was priest of God Most High" (Genesis 14:18). Melchizedek, the king of the city-state of Jerusalem, was a priest who served the true God in this capacity.

We also have the example of Jethro, Moses' father-in-law (Exodus 2:16). He is described as a priest of Midian and appears to have been a priest of the true God for that area of the country.

At Mount Sinai God established the Levitical priest-hood for the Old Testament church (Exodus 28:1, Numbers 18:1–7). The writer of Hebrews summarizes the credentials and qualifications of the high priest (Hebrews 5:1–4). He was to be a man called by God; he was to make sacrifices for the people; and he was to be a direct descendant of Aaron (cf. 2 Chronicles 26:16–21).

The Old Testament priest, like the prophet, served as a type or picture of the promised Savior. "Christ executeth the office of a priest, in his once offering up of himself a sacrifice to satisfy divine justice, and reconcile us to God, and in making continual intercession for us" (SC, Q/A 25).

The Messianic Priest

Psalm 110:4 prophesied that the Messiah would be a priest. However, this prophecy presents us with a great difficulty: the Messiah was to belong to the tribe of Judah; priests on the other hand had to be members of the tribe of Levi. King Uzziah was struck with leprosy for usurping the role of priest (2 Chronicles 26:16–21). How then could the Messiah fulfill this role when he didn't meet the qualifications?

Hebrews 7:14 alludes to this difficulty. "For it is clear that our Lord descended from Judah, and in regard to that tribe Moses said nothing about priests." Jesus Christ, the descendant of David and the appointed Savior, could not function as a priest according to the Aaronic priesthood. How then does God make the Messiah a priest?

Look again at Psalm 110. David's Messianic son would be a priest "in the order of Melchizedek" (vs. 4). The order of Melchizedek preceded the order of Aaron; it was earlier in the unfolding purposes of God's revelation.

The writer of Hebrews discusses the unique character of Melchizedek's priesthood:

This Melchizedek was king of Salem and priest of God Most High. He met Abraham returning from the defeat of the kings and blessed him, and Abraham gave him a tenth of everything. First, his name means "king of righteousness"; then also, "king of Salem" means "king of peace." Without father or mother, without genealogy, without beginning of days or end of life, like the Son of God he remains a priest forever (Hebrews 7:1–3).

Notice the phrases, "Without father or mother, without genealogy, without beginning of days or end of life." The writer does not mean to suggest that Melchizedek was not really a man. Rather, he is referring to the record given us in Scripture. Why are these phrases important? How does this information about Melchizidek make his priesthood unique? The answer is found in the way an Aaronic priest entered the priesthood. He was a priest because the office belonged to his family. He had to have a family tree that proved him to be a descendant of Aaron. If he was to be high priest, he himself had to be a direct descendant of the high priest. But Melchizedek, the priest of the Most High God, had none of the necessary credentials. His priesthood was unique. In addition, his priesthood was perpetual. Melchizedek did not succeed his father and was not followed by his son. His was an ongoing priesthood that he held totally within himself. Thus, he was a "priest extraordinary."

Therefore a priest in the order of Melchizedek would have to meet two qualifications. In the first place, he must be appointed directly by God. Melchizedek was a priest not because of his family, but because God laid his hand on him. He was appointed by the oath of God. God said, "Melchizedek, I appoint you to be a priest."

Now, can God do that? Yes! The church is God's church, and he can appoint anybody he wants to be a priest. For example, God appointed Samuel, who was of the tribe of Ephraim, to function as a priest (1 Samuel 7:9, 10). Thus, Jesus Christ is a priest in the order of Melchizedek because he received his priesthood not from family—he was of the tribe of Judah—but by the direct appointment of the oath of God (Hebrews 7:20, 21).

Second, a priest in the order of Melchizedek must be a single individual, not one of a line of people. Melchizedek's priesthood was personal. He possessed it personally in himself, with no succession. He was a type of Christ, who received his priesthood by the power of an indestructible life:

> And what we have said is even more clear if another priest like Melchizedek appears, one who has become a priest not on the basis of a regulation as to his ancestry (that was the law of Aaron) but on the basis of an indestructible life (Hebrews 7:15, 16).

The writer adds in verse 24, "But because Jesus lives forever, he has a permanent priesthood." Christ was priest because of God's oath and because of his own eternal character. He did not need to belong to an order of priests that had ancestors and descendants, because within himself, having life eternal—indestructible life—he fulfilled all the necessary requirements of the priesthood.

Therefore, Christ is a priest according to the order of Melchizedek. Thus he is a better priest, a priest superior to the Aaronic priests.

Christ's Work as Priest

A priest had two important tasks: to pray for his people and to offer sacrifices for their sins. How did Christ fulfill his priestly office?

While on earth, Jesus prayed for his people. Sometimes we forget about his work of intercessory prayer. Christ's life was marked by its prayerfulness. Of course he prayed for himself (Hebrews 5:7), but he prayed for his people as well. As the perfect priest, he sympathized with the weakness of his people and prayed for them. He became one with us in order to help us through our weaknesses (Hebrews 4:15).

We find a tender example of this in Luke 22:31, 32: "Simon, Simon, Satan has asked to sift you as wheat. But I have prayed for you, Simon, that your faith may not fail. And when you have turned back, strengthen your brothers." Simon was going to be buffeted by Satan, but he would be sustained and preserved by Christ's prayer.

Another beautiful example of Christ's praying on earth for his church is in John 17. He prays for the protection, sanctification, love and unity of his people.

The second aspect of his priestly work on earth was the offering of his life as a sacrifice for the sin of his people. The book of Hebrews graphically describes the way that Jesus, as priest, offered his perfect life to God (Hebrews 7:27). Since his was the complete and ultimate sacrifice, it did not have to be repeated.

In offering himself, Christ fulfilled everything pictured and demanded by the Old Testament sacrificial system. Notice how the work of the high priest on the Day of Atonement paralleled the priestly work of Christ:

When Christ came as high priest of the good things that are already here, he went through the greater and more perfect tabernacle that is not man-made, that is to say, not a part of this creation. He did not enter by means of the blood of goats and calves; but he entered the Most Holy Place once for all by his own blood, having obtained eternal redemption. The blood of goats and bulls and the ashes of a heifer sprinkled on those who are ceremonially unclean sanctify them so that they are outwardly clean. How much more, then, will the blood of Christ, who through the eternal Spirit offered himself un-blemished to God, cleanse our consciences from acts that lead to death, so that we may serve the living God! (Hebrews 9:11–14).

When the high priest annually entered the Holy of Holies, he went with blood for himself and the people. In contrast, our high priest entered not into a man-made Holy of Holies, but into the presence of the eternal God. He entered not with the blood of animals, but with his own blood. The writer of Hebrews concludes, "So Christ was sacrificed once to take away the sins of many people; and he will appear a second time, not to bear sin, but to bring salvation to those who are waiting for him" (Hebrews 9:28). He offered himself as the true sin offering of his people and fulfilled his earthly office of priest.

However, Christ's priestly work did not cease with his earthly ministry. Although some relegate Christ's priestly work to earth and his kingly ministry to heaven, this is not the case at all. Christ exercised all of his offices on earth and continues to do so now from heaven.

The entrance of the Aaronic high priest into the Holy of Holies pictures Christ's entrance into heaven as our priest. The Aaronic high priest had bells on the bottom of his garment. As long as the people heard those bells, they knew he was accepted and not struck dead. As long as *he* was accepted, *they* were accepted, for he bore their names across his chest and upon his shoulders. He went in on their behalf.

Christ, our high priest, took his completed sacrifice into the true Holy of Holies at his ascension (Hebrews 4:14). Furthermore, we are told that when he came into the presence of God he sat down (Hebrews 8:1). The other high priests dared not sit down. They were there temporarily, only once a year. But our high priest sat down because his work is finished. He sits down forever at the right hand of God on behalf of his people. Therefore our hope, our confidence, is within the Holy of Holies (Hebrews 6:19, 20). Our hope and confidence are sure because Christ, our priest, is there. When God accepted *him*, he accepted *you and me*, if we are in a personal union with him. His being in God's presence guarantees that we will be accepted into God's presence.

Christ our high priest, having entered into the Holy of Holies, continues to pray for us. The Bible teaches that he is at the right hand of God making intercession for us. "Who is he that condemns? Christ Jesus, who died—more than that, who was raised to life—is at the right hand of God and is also interceding for us" (Romans 8:34; cf. Hebrews 7:25). Christ is praying for us right now in a way similar to what he did on earth. The difference is that now he is asking for that which he purchased. His are the requests of the honored Son who has been told, "Ask of me, and I will make the nations your inheritance" (Psalm 2:8). He asks as the victor, as the heir who is coming into his inheritance; everything that he asks for as the glorified Son is his.

His prayer is first of all judicial prayer. The Bible pictures Satan accusing us, demanding our condemnation because we are sinners. However, Christ stands on our behalf and says, "Yes, they are sinners; yes, they've done everything you've said they've done and a lot more; yes, they deserve to be sent to hell, and in fact, they were. I took their place." Charles Wesley wrote,

> Five bleeding wounds he bears,
> Received on Calvary;
> They pour effectual prayers,
> They strongly plead for me;
> Forgive him, O forgive, they cry,
> Forgive him, O forgive, they cry,
> Nor let that ransomed sinner die!
> (*Trinity Hymnal*, 223)

He took our place. Thus he can say, "Be gone, Satan, because *they* have paid the penalty *in me*."

Second, it is sanctifying prayer, similar to what he prays

in John 17. He claims for us the benefits that he has purchased: strength in our weakness, victory over sin and conformity to his image. All these things are ours because Christ is praying for us.

Shouldn't we pray for the things for which he is praying? "Lord, give me the holiness that you have purchased for me." We can pray with great boldness, for we know that Christ himself is seeking this for us.

Finally, it is mediatorial prayer. He is making our prayers acceptable (Revelation 8:3–5). This passage pictures the prayers of Christ mingling with those of the church so that their prayers might be acceptable to God. Our prayers are tainted and imperfect because of our sin; but every prayer that we offer in Christ is made perfect by him. Just as God justifies us for the sake of Christ, so he accepts our prayers because we belong to his Son. For this reason we can be confident that God hears us. Christ has perfected our prayers and guarantees them by making them his prayers as well. This is why we pray in his name.

What a comfort it is to know that Christ is our priest! He has reconciled God to us by his atoning work. Our sins are forgiven, and we come boldly into the presence of God. In Christ our priest we live and move and have our being. He communicates to us the grace, the strength and the comfort of his work. He guarantees our access to God and the acceptance of our prayers.

Review Questions

1. Why does every person need a priest?

2. From what tribe did the priesthood come in the Old Testament church?

3. How could the Messiah, who was to be from the tribe of Judah, fulfill the role of priest?

4. Who was Melchizedek, and how was Christ a priest in the order of Melchizedek?

5. What two priestly functions did Christ perform while on earth?

6. What is Christ doing now as our great High Priest?

Discussion Questions

1. Why do you think Abel's offering was accepted and Cain's wasn't?

2. One of the great Reformed distinctives is the priesthood of believers. Discuss how the priesthood of Christ makes each of his people a priest.

3. How does a knowledge of Christ's work as priest affect our praying and worshiping?

9

BEHOLD THE LAMB OF GOD

He was an amazing man. Like a meteor, suddenly he appeared, proclaiming the necessity of repentance. People flocked to him from all quarters, and he gathered a large number of faithful disciples. However, there was a restlessness about him; he seemed to be looking for someone or something. But then one day, as he was speaking to his disciples, John the Baptist saw a figure approaching them. Choosing his words with care, John announced, "Behold the Lamb of God who is to take away the sin of the world."

John knew that his search was over—the Savior had come! With these words he pointed men to the Messiah, the one who would fulfill what the Old Testament sacrifices pictured; the one who would provide the sacrifice that actually takes away sin.

John's announcement turns our attention to the second aspect of the priestly work of Christ—his offering himself as a sacrifice for sinners. In the previous chapter, we considered Christ's work as our high priest, a priest after the order of Melchizedek. But in addition to being the priest, Christ is also the sacrifice. As the Lamb of God, Jesus Christ fulfilled all the animal sacrifices:

> When Christ came as high priest of the good things that are already here, he went through the greater and more perfect tabernacle that is not man-made, that is to say, not a part of this creation. He did not enter by means of the blood of goats

and calves; but he entered the Most Holy Place once for all by his own blood, having obtained eternal redemption. The blood of goats and bulls and the ashes of a heifer sprinkled on those who are ceremonially unclean sanctify them so that they are outwardly clean. How much more, then, will the blood of Christ, who through the eternal Spirit offered himself unblemished to God, cleanse our consciences from acts that lead to death, so that we may serve the living God! (Hebrews 9:11–14).

He was the ultimate vicarious, substitutionary sacrifice.

In this chapter we will examine Christ's work against the backdrop of the Old Testament, using these three categories: Christ the vicarious sacrifice, Christ the sinless sacrifice, and Christ the propitiatory sacrifice.

Christ the Vicarious Sacrifice

The Old Testament sacrificial animals were *vicarious* sacrifices. This means that the animals were *substitutes*. The animal stood in a special relationship to the person offering it; what should have been done to the person was done instead to the animal.

When the offerer laid his hand on the head of the sacrificial victim, this action signified that the victim took the place of the offerer: "He is to lay his hand on the head of the burnt offering, and it will be accepted on his behalf to make atonement for him" (Leviticus 1:4). And in fact the sin, the guilt of the offerer, was in a sense imputed to—that is, placed upon—the victim. As long as the sacrificial system was in effect, God dealt with his people by this vicarious, substitutionary relationship.

As the Savior, Christ was appointed by God to be the vicarious representative of his people. Isaiah 53:4–10 tells us that he was crushed and destroyed for the sins of his people. Paul summarizes this for us in 2 Corinthians 5:21: "God made him who had no sin to be sin for us." We call this *imputation*. Christ took upon himself the guilt of our sin.

This is graphically pictured for us by Martin Luther in his commentary on Galatians 3:13—

> But Christ took all our sins upon him, and for them died upon the cross: therefore it behoved that he should become a transgressor, and (as Isaiah saith, chap. 53) 'to be reckoned among transgressors.' And this, no doubt, all the prophets did foresee in spirit, that Christ should become the greatest transgressor, murderer, adulterer, thief, rebel, blasphemer, &c. that ever was or could be in all the world. For he being made a sacrifice for the sins of the whole world, is not now an innocent person and without sins, is not now the Son of God born of the Virgin Mary; but a sinner, which hath and carrieth the sin of Paul, who was a blasphemer, an oppressor and a persecutor; of Peter, which denied Christ; of David, which was an adulterer, a murderer, and caused the Gentiles to blaspheme the name of the Lord: and briefly, which hath and beareth all the sins of all men in his body, that he might make satisfaction for them with his own blood.

Now, for someone to be a fit substitute, there must be an appropriate relationship. In baseball a pinch hitter must be a player on the same team as the one whose place he will take. Therefore the blood of bulls and goats could not atone for man's sin—the substitute for a human being had to be himself a man. It was for this reason the Son of God became a man.

But the transaction that made Jesus a fit substitute did not originate with the incarnation. The key to the transaction is found in our union with Christ so aptly expressed by the phrase *in him*. Christ was the substitute for those "in him," and this union was established in eternity:

Praise be to the God and Father of our Lord Jesus Christ, who has blessed us in the heavenly realms with every spiritual blessing in Christ. For he chose us in him before the creation of the world to be holy and blameless in his sight. In love he predestined us to be adopted as his sons through Jesus Christ, in accordance with his pleasure and will—to the praise of his glorious grace, which he has freely given us in the One he loves (Ephesians 1:3–5).

We are in Christ *by the covenant*. Christ is our covenant head. God appointed him to act on behalf of those whom he would save. In eternity, when God chose his people, he chose us in Christ, which means he gave us to Christ. The eternal Son of God stepped forward and offered himself as the mediator of his elect. We were placed in union with him because he is our promised Redeemer.

Because we are in Christ covenantally, we were in him *practically*. This is sometimes called the mystical union. On the basis of this union, Paul states in Romans 6:3, 4 that we died in Christ and were raised with Christ. Because he died and was raised as our substitute, we in a sense were *with* him. It is as if *we* died and were raised.

This union is made ours personally *by conversion*. When the Holy Spirit regenerates us and we trust in Christ, we are joined to him and begin to experience the dynamic vitality of Christ's resurrection power.

Thus Christ is our vicarious sacrifice. As the Old Testament believer placed his hands on the head of the sacrificial victim, thereby symbolically transferring his sin to the animal, so God laid the guilt of our sin on Christ. Christ then acted on our behalf. What he did in his obedience, suffering and death, he did for his people as their substitute. He was the vicarious, substitutionary sacrifice.

Christ the Sinless Sacrifice

Christ was also the sinless sacrifice. Theologians use two terms to describe Christ's obedience: his *active obedience* and his *passive obedience*. By his active obedience Christ fulfilled every requirement of God's law; by his passive obedience Christ offered himself as the sacrifice for our sins. It is his active obedience that makes him the sinless sacrifice.

The Old Testament sacrifices had to be physically perfect:

> Do not bring anything with a defect, because it will not be accepted on your behalf. When anyone brings from the herd or flock a fellowship offering to the LORD to fulfill a special vow or as a freewill offering, it must be without defect or blemish to be acceptable. Do not offer to the LORD the blind, the injured, or the maimed, or anything with warts or festering or running sores. Do not place any of these on the altar as an offering made to the LORD by fire. You may, however, present as a freewill offering an ox or a sheep that is deformed or stunted, but it will not be accepted in fulfillment of a vow. You must not offer to the LORD an animal whose testicles are bruised, crushed, torn or cut. You must not do this in your own land, and you must not accept such animals from the hand of a foreigner and offer them as the food of your God. They will not be accepted on your behalf, because they are deformed and have defects (Leviticus 22:20–25).

The sacrificial victim could have no deformities; it had to be without blemish. It was to be as physically perfect as an animal could be.

The physical perfection described in the Old Testament pictured the moral perfection of the Savior. Christ, as the perfect sacrifice, was to be morally perfect, without blemish. In Chapter 5, we dealt with the sinlessness of Christ. Hebrews 9:14 indicates the importance of his sinlessness to his work as our vicarious sacrifice: "How much more, then, will the blood of Christ, who through the eternal Spirit offered himself unblemished to God . . ." Peter tells us that Christ was "a lamb without blemish or defect" (1 Peter 1:19).

So the Christ who offered himself for us was the unblemished sacrifice. In order to be this kind of sacrifice he had to fulfill the law of God perfectly. Hebrews 10:4–9 informs us that Christ came to earth with the intention of fulfilling absolutely the law of God. Paul had this same truth in view when he wrote, "But when the time had fully come, God sent his Son, born of a woman, born under the law, to redeem those under law" (Galatians 4:4).

Christ fulfilled the ceremonial requirements of the law. When John the Baptist hesitated to baptize Jesus, Jesus said, "Let it be so now; it is proper for us to do this to fulfill all righteousness" (Matthew 3:15). In order to identify with his people, Christ had to be baptized, just as he had to be circumcised, even though he had no original sin.

Jesus not only fulfilled the ceremonial aspects of the law, he also perfectly fulfilled the moral demands of the law. In order to be our vicarious sacrifice, Christ had to be sinless. The sinless one was to take the place of sinners. But in addition, we need his obedience if we are to be accepted by God. So often we think of the sacrifice of Christ only in terms of the removal of our guilt. But what would happen if God only removed our guilt? We would be pardoned, but not restored to a right relation with God. Without a positive righteousness, we would not be accepted by God. Christ, by his active obedience, purchased all righteousness for us. Thus by his active obedience he was the sinless sacrifice who paid the penalty of our sins and purchased for us the righteousness of justification.

Christ the Propitiatory Sacrifice

Christ, as well as being the perfect, vicarious sacrifice, is also the *propitiatory* sacrifice. This is what his passive obedience refers to.

The Old Testament sacrifices were *propitiatory*. That is, they were sacrifices designed to remove the wrath of God, cleanse the sinner from the defilement of sin and bring him back into a proper relationship with God. To propitiate someone is to remove his anger and restore favor with him. The sacrifices propitiated God.

In the first six chapters of Leviticus, a number of different sacrificial transactions are described: the burnt offering, sin offering, guilt offering, peace offering and thank offering. Each of these requires the death of the sacrificial victim. In the slaying of the animal, God is declaring that the soul that sins must die. These animals died as atoning, propitiatory sacrifices. They died in the place of God's people.

However, this sacrificial system was never to be an end in itself. The people were to be looking for the Savior to come. As the writer of Hebrews says in the ninth chapter, it should have been obvious to the worshipers that the blood of bulls and goats cannot take away the guilt of sin. As they offered their sacrifices, they were to believe that God would pardon them through the work of the Savior to come. The sacrifices continually held before them the need for that atoning sacrifice.

Jesus Christ fulfilled the Old Testament sacrifices by suffering the wrath of God in our place. Paul tells us that God justifies us on the basis of the propitiatory sacrifice of Jesus Christ (Romans 3:25). When our guilt was imputed to him as our vicarious substitute, God punished him in our place. By the transaction at Calvary, Jesus suffered the eternal punishment of God in order to save his people from that punishment in hell. Thus the wrath of God is removed from us. When we believe in Christ our sins are pardoned, and we are declared righteous.

Now, as the propitiatory sacrifice, Christ fully accomplished the salvation of his people. Once we understand that he was a vicarious and propitiatory sacrifice, we can begin to understand that he absolutely purchased salvation for those whose place he took. We call this "particular redemption." By particular redemption we mean that, when Jesus Christ obeyed, suffered, died and rose from the dead, he acted in a special way for the elect. All those for whom he died will be saved, and he died only for those the Father eternally chose in him. "'You are worthy to take the scroll and to open its seals, because you were slain, and with your blood you purchased men for God from every tribe and language and people and nation'" (Revelation 5:9). You see, he didn't purchase every tribe, tongue, people, and nation, but he purchased men *out of* every tribe, tongue, people, and nation.

This means that Christ's death fully purchased salvation; it didn't simply make salvation possible. If it only made salvation possible, then you and I must do something to complete the transaction. In other words, it would be Christ's work plus our faith that saves us. But this would mean that we contribute something to our salvation; it would be no longer all by God's grace (Romans 11:6).

But the Bible does not depict faith as something we do to complete our salvation. Rather, Christ suffered and died in a saving way for those whom the Father gave him. Christ is the sinless, vicarious, propitiatory sacrifice, who absolutely and completely purchased the salvation of his people.

Review Questions

1. What three aspects of Old Testament sacrifices are pictures of Christ's atoning work?

2. How is Christ a vicarious sacrifice?

3. What aspect of Christ's obedience teaches that he is sinless?

4. What is meant by our union with Christ?

5. What is meant by Christ's passive obedience in his work as our sacrifice?

6. For whom did Christ die? Give biblical evidence to prove that Jesus Christ died for the sins of his elect people.

Discussion Questions

1. What comfort is the active obedience of Jesus Christ to the Christian facing death?

2. What does the concept of union with Christ teach us about election and the relation of election to Christ's atoning work?

3. Why is it important to understand that Christ died for his people and not for all men?

4. Does the doctrine of particular redemption hinder aggressive evangelism? Defend your answer.

10

THE GREAT KING

The tension had been building. A usurper was on the throne, and the true king had come to reclaim it. A number of skirmishes had taken place, but the true king had refrained from making his intentions public. Now, however, he was ready to declare himself king by marching on the capital. Gathering his followers in a village a few miles from the capital city, he made his move. You can find the description of this scene in Matthew 21:1–11. We usually refer to this event as Jesus' triumphal entry.

The Shorter Catechism tells us that, in accomplishing our redemption, Christ executes the offices of prophet, priest and king. Having examined his work as prophet and priest, we turn our attention to his work as our great king.

Reclaiming His Throne

Jesus Christ came as the messianic king. Note that the term *messiah* means "the anointed one." In the mind of the Jews this title, above all else, implied kingship. The triumphal entry is Jesus' public declaration of his kingship.

This is a public declaration because Jesus deliberately fulfilled a messianic prophecy. Zechariah had prophesied that the messianic king would come to Jerusalem mounted on the foal of a donkey (9:9). By entering Jerusalem in this manner, Jesus was pointing the spotlight on himself and saying, "I am the promised king."

Jesus had been somewhat reticent to refer to himself as the king of the Jews. The Jews were looking for a messiah who would come with the might of David and Solomon and overthrow the Roman Empire. If Jesus had referred to himself as Messiah or the Son of David, it would have stirred up all the wrong expectations concerning him. So he was quite hesitant to do so. As king, he had come to overthrow Satan, not Herod and the Romans. Satan was the usurper on the throne.

During most of his ministry Jesus did not draw attention to the truth that he was the messianic king. But the gospel writers, especially Matthew, writing after Jesus accomplished his earthly work, clearly demonstrate that he came to establish the messianic kingdom. Matthew begins his gospel, saying, "A record of the genealogy of Jesus Christ the son of David, the son of Abraham" (1:1). The genealogy gives the legal proof that Jesus of Nazareth was the son of David and establishes the foundation for the fact that he was the Davidic king.

Matthew takes every opportunity to point out that Jesus fulfilled the Old Testament messianic prophecies. For example, he points out that Jesus was born in Bethlehem, the city in which the messianic king was to be born (2:5, 6). He also quotes the words with which Jesus began his public ministry: "Repent, for the kingdom of heaven is at hand" (4:17). The emphasis on repentance shows that he did not come to overthrow Herod and Caesar but to overthrow Satan and establish the messianic kingdom.

All of this comes to a climax in the triumphal entry. Notice that the symbolism of this action was not lost on the Jews. They shouted out, "Hosanna to the Son of David" (Matthew 21:9). But the mere fact that Jesus rode into Jerusalem on a donkey's colt did not mean his claim to be the

Messiah was valid. Anybody can have a parade! What evidence exists to support Jesus' claim to be the messianic king?

Jesus' miracles establish his messianic credentials. Near the end of his Gospel, John wrote:

> Jesus did many other miraculous signs in the presence of his disciples, which are not recorded in this book. But these are written that you may believe that Jesus is the Christ, the Son of God, and that by believing you may have life in his name (John 20:30, 31).

John is saying, "I recorded the miracles so that you will be convinced that he is who he claimed to be."

Jesus himself referred to his miracles in a similar way. "I have testimony weightier than that of John. For the very work that the Father has given me to finish, and which I am doing, testifies that the Father has sent me" (John 5:36). Anybody can go into a telephone booth and put on a Superman costume. But we will not believe that he is Superman unless he can do the works of Superman. Only if he flies, or leaps tall buildings in a single bound, will we concede that he is Superman. Well, in the days of Christ anybody could say, "I am the Messiah." In fact, a number of people did so. But they were not to be believed unless they did the works of the Messiah. Jesus, in performing the miracles given to him by the Father, verified his claim to be the king of the Jews.

We are dealing with miracles at this point in our study because they were primarily a demonstration of Christ's kingship. His mediatorial kingship, in a sense, did not begin until his resurrection and ascension. At that time, he entered fully into his rule. However, the authority that Christ exercised through his miracles established that he was indeed the messianic king. He had an absolute authority over all things, physical and spiritual.

Let's take just one example of Jesus' power over the *physical world*. We could talk about any number of things, from healing lepers and opening the eyes of the blind to restoring withered limbs and causing the lame to walk. But all of us would agree that the greatest of Christ's miracles was raising the dead. Among the many examples of his raising the dead, the one that stands out above all others is the resurrection of Lazarus, who had been dead four days (John 11:30–44).

By calling Lazarus out of the tomb, Jesus clearly demonstrated his kingly authority over death. However, we must not forget that miracles were part of Jesus' battle with the usurper. The Savior's power over the physical world demonstrates that his kingdom will bring full restoration. Jesus will undo all the evil influences of the usurper. He will restore right order in the world, and we will live with him forever in perfectly restored bodies.

Furthermore, his miracles manifested his *spiritual authority*. The great spiritual contest was, of course, with Satan. The miracles illustrated the great truths of conversion: the spiritually dead would be made alive, the spiritually blind would see, for example. But they were more than spiritual illustrations. The Savior was doing battle with Satan for the hearts and minds of men. He showed his spiritual authority by casting out demons.

Satan sought to thwart Christ by having the demons physically possess people. Christ showed his kingly authority by casting the demons out. This is clearly seen in Matthew 12. Jesus is accused of casting out demons by the power of Satan. In response to that accusation, he says, "If I drive out demons by the Spirit of God, then the kingdom of God has come upon you. Or again, how can anyone enter a strong man's house and carry off his possessions unless he first ties up the strong man? Then he can rob his house" (Matthew 12:28, 29). Do you see what Jesus is claiming? The messianic kingship! As he casts out demons, he declares that his kingdom has come into their midst. God's king has come to do battle with the kingdom of darkness. He has bound the strong man and is plundering his kingdom. He has come to release men and women from the bondage of sin by making them sons and daughters of God. Jesus demonstrated his kingship by his miracles.

Jesus came to reclaim the kingdom. At the fall, Satan usurped the kingdom of the world. Christ came to win it back. The defeating blow, of course, was struck by his death and resurrection. On the cross Christ entered into hand-to-hand combat with Satan and was declared the victor by the resurrection. Having won back the throne, Christ is now exalted at the right hand of God as the great King.

Jesus' Present Rule

By his resurrection and ascension, Jesus was given absolute authority. He now rules over all things. Having defeated Satan, the prince of this world, Jesus came into his full crowned rights. He asserts, "All authority in heaven and on earth has been given to me. Therefore go and make disciples" (Matthew 28:18). He is saying, "Because all authority has been given to me in heaven and on earth, go make disciples of all nations." The church's mission in the world is based upon Christ's kingly authority, and that is an absolute authority. All authority is given to him in heaven and on earth. Nothing has been exempted.

But we need to understand that Christ is reigning *now*.

Christ's kingly rule is not postponed until he begins a thousand-year reign upon the earth. Regardless of our view of the millennium (whether or not Christ will physically reign on the earth for a thousand years), we all must recognize that Jesus Christ is now on the throne and ruling.

In ruling, Christ exercises the three great functions listed in the Shorter Catechism, Q/A 26. "How doth Christ execute the office of a king? Christ executeth the office of a king, in subduing us to himself, in ruling and defending us, and in restraining and conquering all his and our enemies."

First, he subdues his people to himself. In other words, he is converting the lost. He is actively gathering his elect. In his kingly work he applies to the unconverted all that he has accomplished. Christ, the priest, having provided a perfect salvation through his own redeeming work, is praying now for his elect to be brought to him. As prophet he calls them by his Word. As king he exercises his saving power and through his Word applies his priestly work and draws sinners to himself. David points this out, "Your troops [people] will be willing on your day of battle. Arrayed in holy majesty, from the womb of the dawn you will receive the dew of your youth" (Psalm 110:3).

As Christ rules in the midst of his enemies, he converts enemies into sons and friends. One of the most beautiful examples of this is the conversion of Saul of Tarsus. Saul hated Christ and his church. But when Jesus laid hold of him, he said, "What shall I do, Lord?" (Acts 22:10). Saul was conquered by the risen Christ. Notice that Saul was not given a choice. He did not exercise any so-called free will. He said, "Lord, what would you have me to do?" because Christ had revealed himself as king.

Now, when we say that as king Christ subdues his

people to himself, we do not imply that he is a tyrannical king who forcibly makes people his unwilling captives. Not at all. Jesus, by the work of the Holy Spirit, makes his people willing. The Spirit of God, upon the commandment of King Jesus, changes the heart of the individual. This is called the new birth. And because of this new birth, when the king says, "Come and follow me," the changed individual replies, "Yes, Lord, what must I do?"

The reality of Christ's rule ought to make the church enthusiastic about the cause of Christ. Many are now pessimistic. But we should remember that Christ is on the throne. The nations have been given to him as an inheritance (Psalm 2:8). All authority in heaven and on earth is his (Matthew 28:18). Satan has been defeated (Revelation 12:10, 11). The elect are being gathered in and the nations discipled. Christ is conquering through his church!

Second, Christ rules and defends us. Christ our king is our Lord and Master. After Jesus washed the disciples' feet, he sat down and said, "You call me 'Teacher' and 'Lord,' and rightly so, for that is what I am. Now that I, your Lord and Teacher, have washed your feet, you also should wash one another's feet" (John 13:13, 14). Because he is Lord and Master we are to follow his example. And we find his example, not only in his *life*, but also in his *law*. He rules over us by his Word. Jesus says, "If you love me, you will obey what I command" (John 14:15). Because he is our Lord, we want to obey him. He says, "My sheep listen to my voice . . . and they follow me" (John 10:27). How do we follow him? We follow him by obeying his Word.

As our Lord and Master, he also defends us. He is actively protecting us. He guarantees that our lives are safe in the palm of his hand until the day he brings us into his glorious presence.

A brief note is in order here. Since Jesus is Lord over all those he subdues, no Christian can have Jesus only as Savior and not as Lord. Because as king he converts us, our response will always be the response of Paul: "Lord, what would you have me to do?" There is no such thing as a class of converted people who are living as unconverted people and do not yet have Jesus as Lord. Of course, none of us is perfect. We sin; we wrestle with sin; we backslide; we can live carnally in certain areas of our lives for certain periods of time. But the "carnal Christian" as defined by some people today does not exist. If Christ is our Savior, he rules us.

Third, Christ restrains and conquers his and our enemies by holding them back through judgments and the restraining work of the Holy Spirit. An example of this is found in the book of Esther. Haman hated God's people. Early one morning he came to the palace to ask the king to hang the Jew, Mordecai. But the king, afflicted with insomnia, had been reading the record of his reign and discovered that Mordecai had saved his life. In the course of the interview, the king said, "Haman, what shall I do for the man who has been loyal and faithful to me?" Haman thought the king was talking about him and designed a wonderful plan of personal exaltation. Then the king said, "That is great, Haman; take Mordecai the Jew and do for him all that you have said." What a wonderful example of God's restraining and defeating the enemy of his people!

Another example is found in Job 1:1–2:10. Just as Satan couldn't hurt Job without God's permission, so nothing can happen to a Christian or to the church apart from the loving permission of the king. God watches over us to protect us.

Of course, ultimately all enemies will be destroyed. Paul confirms this in 1 Corinthians 15:20–28, where he describes the culmination of the mediatorial kingdom. Referring to Christ as mediatorial king, Paul shows that, when he subdues all enemies, the kingdom will then be handed over to God the Father. No longer will the mediatorial office be needed. But while the church remains on earth, Christ continues to exercise this office.

Christ's office of mediatorial king guarantees the absolute defeat of Satan. Satan has been defeated on the cross, and now he is writhing in his death agony. Although the Devil still has a great deal of strength, Christ's foot is already on his neck, and he will be cast into hell for eternity.

This victory over Satan also includes the defeat of death. Paul exclaims,

> When the perishable has been clothed with the imperishable, and the mortal with immortality, then the saying that is written will come true: "Death has been swallowed up in victory." "Where, O death is your victory? Where, O death, is your sting?" (1 Corinthians 15:54, 55).

And, of course, Christ the king will eventually destroy all of the unrighteous. All who remain impenitent will be cast into hell for eternity.

We have surveyed only a little of what Scripture says about Christ our king. These truths should fill us with a great deal of delight, as well as comfort, as we see Christ on his throne exercising all authority on our behalf.

Review Questions

1. What is Jesus declaring in his triumphal entry?

2. How did Jesus demonstrate his kingship during his earthly ministry?

3. How did the miracles demonstrate Jesus' physical authority? his spiritual authority?

4. How does Jesus subdue his people?

5. In what way does Jesus Christ rule and defend his people?

6. How is he presently restraining his enemies?

7. When will the final conquest be completed?

Discussion Questions

1. If the primary purpose of miracles was to validate the claim that Jesus of Nazareth is the Messiah, and since they are recorded in the Bible, is there a need today for people to be able to perform miracles?

2. What is the "carnal Christian" theory? How does the kingship of Jesus disprove it?

3. Since Christ is on the throne, what should the church's attitude be to its mission mandate?

4. How does the conversion of Saul of Tarsus illustrate Jesus' kingly rule? What does Saul's conversion teach about the so-called free will of the sinner to chose or reject Jesus Christ?

11

A MORALITY PLAY

There was an awkward silence as the men looked around at one another, wondering what was going to occur. Their leader had been making some very strange statements concerning the future; several in the group had made some power plays for control and leadership. Because of the awkwardness and the fear involved in the situation, the men had not observed the proper principles of etiquette. All were aware of what should be done, but they just sat uncomfortably. Suddenly, their leader got up and did what they should have done. He washed their feet!

Perhaps you recognize in this little narrative the events of John 13. The disciples were bewildered at Jesus' teaching about his suffering and death. Moreover, they did not trust one another. Failing to grasp the central focus of Jesus' ministry, they had earlier argued among themselves about who was greatest (Mark 9:33, 34), and two of them, John and James, had attempted to get the places of preeminence in the group (Mark 10:35–37).

John 13 is an action parable that addressed both their concern for preeminence and their misunderstanding of Jesus' ministry. When Jesus washed the disciples' feet, he made a statement about priorities and values. He taught the disciples that, rather than arguing over who was greatest, they ought to be concerned about serving each other. He concluded,

"Do you understand what I have done for you?" he asked them. "You call me 'Teacher' and 'Lord,' and rightly so, for that is what I am. Now that I, your Lord and Teacher, have washed your feet, you also should wash one another's feet. I have set for you an example that you should do as I have done for you" (John 13:12–15).

The foot-washing was also a profound theological statement. The disciples were confused because they couldn't relate the concept of a glorified messiah to Jesus' preoccupation with rejection and death. Nothing fit. So Jesus washed their feet, and his actions (especially in verses 4, 5 and 12) are a morality play picturing his entire earthly ministry. Jesus laid aside his glory and humbled himself as a servant in order to cleanse and redeem his people from sin and purchase their sanctification. When he completed this work, he returned to his place of glory and honor. In other words, in this morality play Jesus pictures his humiliation and exaltation.

Up to this point we have looked at Christ's work under the concept of his mediatorial offices. As our Savior, he is prophet, priest and king. Under these three headings we have examined his work before his incarnation, on the earth and now in heaven. Another way to look at the work of Christ is through what the catechism calls the humiliation and exaltation of Jesus.

The Shorter Catechism, Q/A 27 describes Christ's humiliation:

Wherein did Christ's humiliation consist? Christ's humiliation consisted in his being born, and that in a low condition, made under the law, undergoing the miseries of this life, the wrath of God, and the cursed death of the cross; in being buried, and continuing under the power of death for a time.

Humiliation in Birth

We may define the concept of humiliation as giving up one's privileges, authority, and honor. What Jesus did is summarized by Paul in Philippians 2:5–8:

> Your attitude should be the same as that of Christ Jesus: Who, being in very nature God, did not consider equality with God something to be grasped, but made himself nothing, taking the very nature of a servant, being made in human likeness. And being found in appearance as a man, he humbled himself and became obedient to death—even death on a cross!

Note the parallel to John 13, our morality play, where Jesus gives up the honor of host and head of the table to perform the menial task of washing the feet of his followers. Jesus Christ, eternally the Son of God, who had every right to remain only God and to be recognized in the full splendor and display of that glory, did not cling to the prerogatives of his Godhead, but rather laid aside its privileges to take on human nature (illustrated when Jesus washed his disciple's feet). This is what we mean by humiliation.

How then did Christ suffer humiliation in his birth? His humiliation "consisted in his being born, and that in a low condition" (SC, Q/A 27). The Larger Catechism spells this out for us in greater detail in Q/A 47:

> How did Christ humble himself in his conception and birth? Christ humbled himself in his conception and birth, in that, being from all eternity the Son of God, in the bosom of the Father, he was pleased in the fullness of time to become the Son of man, made of a woman of low estate, and to be born of her; with divers circumstances of more than ordinary abasement.

It is difficult for us to grasp the humiliation that was

involved in the incarnation. Even though people are at the top of God's created order, the gulf between the eternal Son of God and man is greater than the distance between man and a cockroach. Roaches are despicable creatures, and the thought of having to become a roach would be repulsive. That is just a hint of what it meant for God to become a man. True, man is made in the image of God and has dignity and honor. Nevertheless, even if man had not sinned, the humiliation would still be unimaginable. For the infinite to become finite, for the eternal to become temporal, for the unchangeable to become changeable—that's the great gulf. We need to appreciate the wonderful self-humiliation of Jesus Christ in becoming a man. The very act of birth was absolutely humbling.

But Christ went beyond that. Not only was he born, he was born in a low condition. The circumstances surrounding his birth were abject and miserable. As if it were not enough for him to become a man, he was born to people on the low rung of the social ladder. His family was impoverished. His cradle was a feeding trough (Luke 2:7). His parents couldn't afford the regular sacrifice at the temple (Luke 2:24; cf. Leviticus 12:8). Furthermore, they became refugees. Because of oppression, they had to flee to a foreign country.

For a king to live among his people in order to learn how they lived would be a tremendous thing. But even more amazing would be the king who, wanting to know the true condition of his people, disguised himself as a peasant and worked alongside them in the field, ate what they ate, and lived in their homes. Jesus did even more than that; he actually became one of us and lived in poverty among us. Jesus, therefore, suffered humiliation in the circumstances of his birth.

Humiliation in Life

The second major area of Christ's humiliation is his life.

How did Christ humble himself in his life? Christ humbled himself in his life, by subjecting himself to the law, which he perfectly fulfilled; and by conflicting with the indignities of the world, temptations of Satan, and the infirmities in his flesh, whether common to the nature of man, or particularly accompanying that his low condition (LC, Q/A 48).

Note that he was obligated to fulfill the law of God. "But when the time had fully come, God sent his Son, born of a woman, born under law, to redeem those under law, that we might receive the full rights of sons" (Galatians 4:4).

For us, law-keeping is a high privilege. If we are born again, we delight in the law of God. We want to obey the Lord, and mourn the fact that we can't obey him as we desire. How then was law-keeping an act of humiliation for the Savior? In terms of morality, in terms of the uprightness of his character, no humiliation was involved in his obeying the moral law. The humiliation arises from the fact that he who was to be the recipient of all obedience had to obey. Even though in his divine nature he is worthy to receive obedience, in his human nature he must actively render to God that which should be rendered to himself as the Son of God.

Furthermore, there are aspects of the Ten Commandments that are not binding on God in the same way that they are on us. God has the right to strike dead any of his enemies whenever he wants to; he is not breaking the sixth commandment to do so. However, the Lord Jesus Christ in his human nature as the God-man did not have the authority to take the law into his own hands. That is why his disciples had to sheathe their swords or refrain from calling down fire on the Samaritans. You see, he was to live under the system of God-ordained authority and law. He was in perfect submission to that law.

Moreover, he was in submission to the ceremonial law. Although Jesus Christ was not born with original sin, he was circumcised (Luke 2:21). Even though he had no sins for which to repent, he went to John the Baptist to be baptized (Matthew 3:13). Also, he paid the temple tax. He pointed out that he didn't need to—he was the Son, and children of the King were not required to pay taxes. But he paid it (Matthew 17:24–27).

Jesus humbled himself in the way he rendered his obedience to the moral law and the fact that he kept all of the commands of the ceremonial law.

In his life he suffered all the miseries that are a result of the fall: "By conflicting with the indignities of the world, temptations of Satan, and infirmities in his flesh, whether common to the nature of man, or particularly accompanying that his low condition" (LC, Q/A 48).

Physically, Christ had no place to call his own; he didn't have a home, a bed. We find him suffering the ravages of the weaknesses of this life. He got tired, hungry and thirsty. He was treated with awful contempt by his enemies. "But I am a worm and not a man, scorned by men and despised by the people. All who see me mock me; they hurl insults, shaking their heads" (Psalm 22:6, 7).

Christ also suffered the spiritual miseries of this life. He was tempted in all points as we are (Hebrews 2:17). He suffered severe temptation (Luke 4:1–13). All the physical infirmities as well as all the spiritual infirmities that we experience in this life because of sin, Christ suffered.

Humiliation in Death and Burial

How did Christ humble himself in his death? Christ humbled himself in his death, in that having been betrayed by Judas, forsaken by his disciples, scorned and rejected by the world, condemned by Pilate, and tormented by his persecutors; having also conflicted with the terrors of death, and the powers of darkness, felt and borne the weight of God's wrath, he laid down his life an offering for sin, enduring the painful, shameful, and cursed death of the cross (LC, Q/A 49).

One of the aspects of Christ's humiliation often over-looked is his public condemnation. He was condemned by the Jews as a blasphemer. Pilate condemned him to the cursed death of the cross. In addition, he endured verbal attacks against him while he was on the cross: "If this is the beloved Son of God in whom he takes delight, why does he not deliver him from the cross?" What a blight on a soul that knew nothing but purity! But worst of all was the fact that God condemned him and left him to die on the cross.

Not only was Christ condemned by God, he was also punished. He suffered both physical and spiritual punishment. "God made him who had no sin to be sin for us, so that in him we might become the righteousness of God" (2 Corinthians 5:21). Paul says he was accursed (Galatians 3:13). He was cursed by God and suffered the ravages of hell, which consist of being separated from God's gracious presence and afflicted with spiritual and physical wrath and torment.

Then, of course, he died. The Prince of Life *died*. He who is himself *life* died. *Life* and *Christ* should be synonymous. For him, dying had to be a deliberate act. He would not have died if he had not let go. He voluntarily died, and his soul and body were torn apart.

113

Furthermore, Jesus suffered death absolutely: he didn't die just for an instant. His soul returned to the Father, but his body was buried. You see, it wasn't enough for him to pay the penalty of hell; he also had to die. He had to suffer the separation of body and soul. To signify the reality of this, he underwent that penal punishment of burial. True, his body was supernaturally kept from any deterioration during that time; but still he was dead and buried and remained under the power of death for a period of time.

The humiliation of Christ's death is summarized by the phrase, "He descended into hell." This phrase is confusing to many people. Neither the Larger Catechism nor the Apostle's Creed intend for us to think that Christ physically went to hell. The statement is a summary of what we have said about his suffering the wrath of God, his death and his burial. It refers to the final events in the humiliation of our Savior.

Thus, as Christ acted out his morality play—the incident with which this chapter began—he was demonstrating his humiliation in birth, life, and death.

As we conclude, let us note two very practical lessons. First, Christ's humiliation is a great motivation to obedience and holiness. As Paul says, "For you know the grace of our Lord Jesus Christ, that though he was rich, yet for your sakes he became poor, so that you through his poverty might become rich" (2 Corinthians 8:9). Paul particularly has in view Christian giving, but the principle set forth in this verse is the great motivating factor in all Christian living. Set before your mind's eye Christ's impoverishing himself to make you rich. When you tire of struggling with sin, when you tire of persecution, when you tire of discipline, then remind yourself that Christ suffered for you immeasurably more than you will ever be called on to suffer. Thus his humiliation is a great motivating principle.

Second, his humiliation is a great pattern to follow. Isn't this the conclusion of the morality play in John 13? "I have set before you an example that you should do as I have done for you" (vs. 15). Paul begins the theological statement of Christ's humiliation in the same way: "Your attitude should be the same as that of Christ Jesus" (Philippians 2:5). We are to humble ourselves. That's not an easy thing to do. We are to humble ourselves before our enemies. We are to be willing to be put down, to be misunderstood, to be defrauded—but it isn't easy. We are to bear personal affront; we are not to carry grudges. We are to forgive, for love covers a multitude of sins. He humbled himself for us. He is the pattern. Follow him and learn to be humble.

Review Questions

1. What two things was Jesus teaching when he washed the disciples' feet?

2. What is meant by Christ's humiliation?

3. How was birth an act of humiliation for Christ?

4. How did Jesus Christ humble himself in keeping the law?

5. What were the miseries Jesus underwent for his people while on earth?

6. Of what did his final humiliation consist?

7. Why did Jesus have to be buried?

8. What two lessons do we learn from this?

Discussion Questions

1. When Jesus washed the disciples' feet he commanded them to follow his example. Does this mean that the church should perform ceremonial foot washing? Defend your answer.

2. The Apostles' Creed says that Jesus descended into hell. Relate this article of belief to Christ's humiliation.

3. Discuss practical ways Christ's humiliation can help you deal with problems in your life.

12

THE CORONATION

Most of us enjoy royal pomp and ceremony. I remember waking my daughter at 4:30 in the morning so she could watch the wedding of Prince Charles and Princess Diana. Normally, she doesn't enjoy getting up in the morning. But that morning she was all eyes—she loved every minute of it!

But the occasion for the greatest amount of royal pomp and ceremony is not a wedding but a coronation. In Revelation 5, John describes a royal coronation. His vision takes us into the throne room of heaven. John sees a visible manifestation of God, who is holding a book or a scroll written on the inside and the outside and sealed with seven seals. "Who is worthy to break the seals and open the scroll?" cries out an angel in a loud voice. When John hears that no one is found worthy to open the book, he weeps (Revelation 5:2–4).

John's concern arises from his conviction that this book is the book of God's decree and providence—the ongoing work of God in accomplishing his redemptive purposes in the vindication of the church. Therefore when John hears that no one is worthy to open the book, he is filled with grief. But as he is weeping, one of the elders says to him, "Do not weep! See, the Lion of the tribe of Judah, the Root of David, has triumphed. He is able to open the scroll and its seven seals" (Revelation 5:5).

Even though there is none found among men who is worthy to open the book, the Lion of Judah, the Messiah, the

Root of David, is qualified. As John turns to look, one would think that he would see Christ in the royal, glorified form in which he appeared in Revelation 1:12–16. Instead he sees a Lamb who has been slain (Revelation 5:6). The Lamb takes the book and prepares to break the seals.

I call this scene the coronation of the Lord Jesus Christ. It is an historical flashback. In the symbolism of the vision, John sees a representation of what occurred on the day of Christ's ascension into heaven. Christ entered into his glory. He was crowned, and to him was given the authority to execute the decrees of God on behalf of the church.

But if this is a coronation, why is Christ pictured as a slain lamb? Why isn't he depicted in the royal imagery of the Lion of Judah? God wants us to see the relationship of Christ's humiliation to his exaltation. Christ reached glory by descending the steps of humiliation. Before he could mount up to the glory on high, he had to suffer as the Lamb for the redemption of his people (see Figure 3).

Having examined Christ's humiliation, we shall look at his exaltation. The Shorter Catechism, Q/A 28 describes the exaltation of Christ:

> Wherein consisteth Christ's exaltation? Christ's exaltation consisteth in his rising again from the dead on the third day, in ascending up into heaven, in sitting at the right hand of God the Father, and in coming to judge the world at the last day.

We shall consider the declaration of victory, the victory parade, and the victor's reward.

Declaration of Victory

When God raised his Son from the dead he declared his victory over his enemies. The fact of the resurrection is

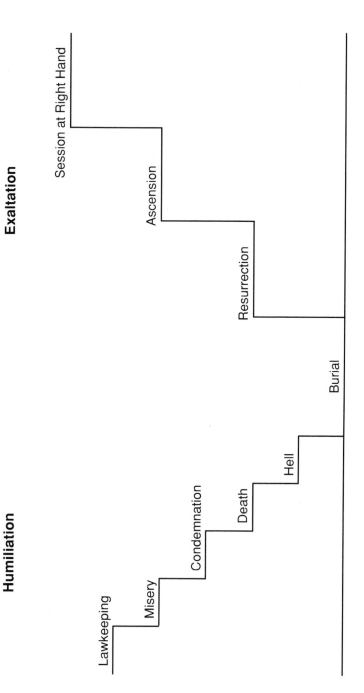

STEPS TO GLORY

Humiliation

Exaltation

Lawkeeping
Misery
Condemnation
Death
Hell
Burial
Resurrection
Ascension
Session at Right Hand

Figure 3

recorded in the Gospels. There is no need to rehearse the events of that Sunday morning, for they are familiar to us all. Simply note that we are talking about an historical event. Jesus Christ, who was dead, was raised from the dead.

Paul speaks of some of the witnesses of the resurrected Christ. Scripture, says Paul, bears witness: "He was buried . . . he was raised on the third day according to the Scriptures" (1 Corinthians 15:4). For example, the resurrection was prophesied in Psalm 16:10.

Furthermore, says Paul, there were many eyewitnesses:

And that he appeared to Peter, and then to the Twelve. After that, he appeared to more than five hundred of the brothers at the same time, most of whom are still living, though some have fallen asleep. Then he appeared to James, then to all the apostles, and last of all he appeared to me also, as to one abnormally born (1 Corinthians 15:5–8).

It is of interest to note that the people to whom he appeared did not expect him to be raised from the dead. The disciples were caught totally off guard by the resurrection. It was not something they expected, nor were they hallucinating. Sometimes in extreme grief a person imagines he sees a dead loved one. This was not the case with the apostles. They touched him, and he ate with them.

Paul himself is the most powerful witness of all, because he was a hostile witness. Before the risen Christ appeared to him, he considered Jesus to be a fraud.

Jesus Christ was raised from the dead. In this act, God vindicated Jesus Christ. Isn't this what Peter is building up to in his Pentecost sermon? Note the contrast:

"This man was handed over to you by God's set purpose

and foreknowledge; and you, with the help of wicked men, put him to death by nailing him to the cross. But God raised him from the dead, freeing him from the agony of death, because it was impossible for death to keep its hold on him" (Acts 2:23, 24).

Peter expands on this:

"Seeing what was ahead, he spoke of the resurrection of the Christ, that he was not abandoned to the grave, nor did his body see decay. God has raised this Jesus to life, and we are all witnesses of the fact" (Acts 2:31, 32).

Paul refers to the resurrection of Christ as a declaration of his victory: "And who through the Spirit of holiness was declared with power to be the Son of God by his resurrection from the dead: Jesus Christ our Lord" (Romans 1:4). His resurrection was a vindication of his life and teaching. It was his victory over his enemies.

You remember that while Jesus was on the cross his enemies taunted him, "If you are God's favored one, come down. If you are the Messiah, deliver yourself! If God loves you, why is he allowing you to go through this terrible, shameful death of the cross?" Jesus suffered all of that mockery in silence. He *couldn't* come down. If he had come down, he would have been disobedient. It was his role to suffer in our place.

Yet his cruel death was a public declaration that he was cursed of God. It appeared to establish his guilt. Would God have allowed his own innocent Son to suffer such abuse and to die? The Jews, therefore, gloated at the defeat of their enemy. Had he remained dead, they would have had every reason to gloat: "Jesus said that he was the Son of God; he committed blasphemy; he deserved to die."

This is why his resurrection is so important: It was his vindication. In the resurrection, God the Father declared that Christ is everything he claimed to be; that he died not for his own guilt, but for the guilt of his people.

In Christ's vindication, *we* are vindicated. Paul says that Christ was "delivered over to death for our sins and was raised to life for our justification" (Romans 4:25). The only reason he was put to death in the first place was because our sins were imputed to him. When he was condemned and executed, we, in him, were condemned and executed. Therefore, his being declared not guilty by the resurrection is the basis of *our* being declared not guilty. His resurrection is the vindication of all those who trust in him, those who are justified by faith alone.

Moreover, Christ's resurrection is the guarantee of *our* resurrection. Paul makes this clear: "For since death came through a man, the resurrection of the dead comes also through a man. For as in Adam all die, so in Christ all will be made alive. That which God did for him he has promised to do for us" (1 Corinthians 15:21, 22). Paul explains more fully:

> We believe that Jesus died and rose again and so we believe that God will bring with Jesus those who have fallen asleep in him. According to the Lord's own word, we tell you that we who are still alive, who are left till the coming of the Lord, will certainly not precede those who have fallen asleep. For the Lord himself will come down from heaven, with a loud command, with the voice of the archangel and with the trumpet call of God, and the dead in Christ will rise first (1 Thessalonians 4:14–16).

The resurrection, therefore, is the first step of exaltation. It is the declaration of victory over sin and death.

The Victory Parade

When a king conquered his enemies, he usually returned to his capital city in a parade that celebrated his victory and displayed its spoils. Christ's victory parade is his ascension, the second aspect of his exaltation. The doctrine of the ascension is frequently lost in the shuffle. The Larger Catechism teaches the significance of the ascension:

> How was Christ exalted in his ascension? Forty days after his resurrection, he, in our nature, and as our head, triumphing over his enemies, visibly went up into the highest heavens, there to receive gifts for men, to raise up our affections thither, and to prepare for us, where himself is, and shall continue till his second coming at the end of the world (Q/A 53).

The ascension was Christ's visible triumph over his enemies as he returned to heaven. The victor returns with the spoils of battle.

David predicts the ascension, using the imagery of a victorious king leading his captives and distributing the plunder to his faithful subjects: "When you ascended on high, you led captives in your train; you received gifts from men, even from the rebellious—that you, O Lord God, might dwell there" (Psalm 68:18).

Luke gives the actual account of the ascension:

> After he said this, he was taken up before their very eyes, and a cloud hid him from their sight. They were looking intently up into the sky as he was going, when suddenly two men dressed in white stood beside them. "Men of Galilee," they said, "Why do you stand here looking into the sky? This same Jesus, who has been taken from you into heaven, will come back in the same way you have seen him go into heaven" (Acts 1:9–11).

This is his victory parade. In ascending, Christ declared his triumph over his enemies. As Paul puts it, "And having disarmed the powers and authorities, he made a public spectacle of them, triumphing over them by the cross" (Colossians 2:15). Therefore, we know our enemy is defeated and our sins are forgiven.

Moreover, as he went on high, he took us as willing captives, led "in triumphal procession in Christ" (2 Corinthians 2:14). Because we are in union with him and our salvation was secured by him, there is a sense in which every Christian was in that victory parade. This is the guarantee that we too shall ascend on high and share in his glory. We shall live with him forever in glorified bodies.

Finally, in the victory parade Jesus received the spoils from which he gathers the gifts to bestow upon his church (Ephesians 4:8–11). On the basis of his completed work, he now gives his church the Holy Spirit and gifts of office and service.

Revelation 5:9–14 captures some of the unrestrained joy of that occasion. All the angels, all the elders representing the church, and all of heaven and earth were praising him. What a day that was! Angels had sung at his descent in humiliation. With how much more joy did they sing when their Captain, whom they had longed to rush forth and defend (Matthew 26:53), returned in glory! The streets of heaven must have been lined with all the souls of those who had gone ahead, along with all the angels of heaven. Every heavenly creature was straining to look at the glorified God-man as he marched right up to the throne of God and received the scroll.

The Victor's Reward

Christ's reward was his crowning as mediatorial King. "The LORD says to my Lord: 'Sit at my right hand until I make your enemies a footstool for your feet'" (Psalm 110:1). This sitting at the right hand of God is the ultimate glorification of the Lord Jesus Christ, the God-man.

It is important that we understand the figure of speech used here. The Bible would not have us think of Jesus as perpetually sitting on a throne. Rather is this an ancient metaphorical expression to show that he has been given supreme authority; God the Father has given to him the execution of all things. That's the significance of the scroll. It symbolizes that Christ's glorification has been accomplished and that he has been given the authority to execute the decrees of God.

When he ascended, he was exalted with divine glory as a reward for his work as Savior (Hebrews 12:2). In a sense, he was crowned. Paul describes this coronation in Philippians 2:9–11:

> Therefore God exalted him to the highest place and gave him the name that is above every name, that at the name of Jesus every knee should bow, in heaven and on earth and under the earth, and every tongue confess that Jesus Christ is Lord, to the glory of God the Father.

Perhaps you are wondering, "To what extent can the Son of God be glorified?" He is the eternal Son of God. He did not give up divinity or divine attributes to become a man. What he *did* give up was the prerogative of being recognized and worshiped as the eternal Son of God. His divine glory was veiled in his humiliation. In his exaltation, nothing new was added to him as the eternal Son of God. He was manifested in all the splendor and glory of the second person of the Godhead.

A second question is, "To what extent does his human nature share in the divine glory?" This is a great mystery. It is the God-man Jesus Christ who is glorified and given the name "Lord" (Philippians 2:9–11). Because of the personal union of his human nature with his divine nature, when his divine nature was exalted and glorified the human nature shared in that glorification. It is as the God-man that he is declared to be Jehovah forever and ever. This is phenomenal. It is the ultimate guarantee that his work is finished.

However, this is not to say that the human nature has received divine attributes. No—that can no more happen now than when he was on the earth. When Christ ascended into heaven, he did not cease being a man. He is still the God-man and always will be. When Christ ascended into heaven as the God-man, although the human nature received divine glory because of its union with the divine, it did not receive divine attributes. For example, his human nature is not omnipresent. He cannot physically be in more than one place at a time.

The divine nature is again manifested in all its splendor and glory. The human nature is glorified in sinless perfection, and because of its union with the divine it receives all glory and honor. As the glorified God-man, Christ Jesus is crowned and enters into his mediatorial reign. He exercises his offices of prophet, priest and king.

Christ is crowned as his reward (Hebrews 12:2) and has earned the right to give the Holy Spirit to his church. Peter says that this is the significance of Pentecost, "Exalted to the right hand of God, he has received from the Father the promised Holy Spirit and has poured out what you now see and hear" (Acts 2:33). In this manner he distributes the spoils to his people.

Furthermore, he is ruling over all things for the sake of the church (Ephesians 1:20–23). Every event that occurs anywhere in the world, small as well as major—everything is being controlled by Christ for the sake of the church. There is not one little thing in all of life that slips out from under that umbrella of authority. He is actively gathering, preserving, and vindicating the elect.

When the last elect person has been converted and brought to that degree of sanctification appointed by God, then Christ shall return, and the perfected church will be handed over to the triune God. Then Christ will cease his role of Mediator. We will still love and worship him as our Savior, but his role of mediation will be accomplished with his second coming.

> How is Christ exalted in his sitting at the right hand of God? Christ is exalted in his sitting at the right hand of God, in that as God-man he is advanced to the highest favor with God the Father, with all fulness of joy, glory, and power over all things in heaven and earth; and doth gather and defend his church, and subdue their enemies; furnisheth his ministers and people with gifts and graces, and maketh intercession for them (LC, Q/A 54).

Review Questions

1. What scene is revealed symbolically to John in Revelation 5?

2. Why is the victorious king pictured as a lamb?

3. What three things did God declare when he raised his son from the dead?

4. What is the significance of the ascension?

5. What does the Bible teach when it says that Christ is at the right hand of God the Father?

6. In what way has the God-man been glorified?

Discussion Questions

1. If Christ reached glory through suffering, what does this teach us about the road to heaven? About the importance of humbling ourselves?

2. What does Paul mean when he says in Ephesians 2:6 that we are seated with Christ in heaven?

3. Lutherans teach that the physical body of Christ is present at every observance of the Lord's Supper. According to them, this can happen because at Christ's glorification his human nature became omnipresent. In light of what you have learned, do you think the glorification of Christ enables his body to participate in divine attributes?

13

THE END!

I am not a detail person. I find it difficult and sometimes boring to tie up the loose ends of a project in order to bring it to a neat conclusion. But God has no loose ends. He completes what he starts. The salvation project begun in eternity will be brought to a perfect conclusion. Jesus Christ the God-man has done everything as prophet, priest and king to secure our salvation. But one more thing must occur. God must write The End on the book of history. This will be accomplished with the last act of the exalted Mediator—the return of the Lord Jesus Christ. The culminating event of Christ's exaltation as the God-man is his second coming.

The Promise of the Second Coming

The second coming is clearly promised in the Scriptures. Christ kept the certainty of this event before the minds of his disciples. For example, he promises, "When the Son of Man comes in his glory, and all the angels with him, he will sit on his throne in heavenly glory" (Matthew 25:31).

This promise is repeated by the angels at his ascension. "Men of Galilee," they said, "why do you stand here looking into the sky? This same Jesus, who has been taken from you into heaven, will come back in the same way you have seen him go into heaven" (Acts 1:11). This theme is reiterated throughout the New Testament. It is Paul's hope:

For what is our hope, our joy, or the crown in which we will

glory in the presence of our Lord Jesus when he comes? . . .
May he strengthen your hearts so that you will be blameless
and holy in the presence of our God and Father when our Lord
Jesus comes with all his holy ones (1 Thessalonians 2:19; 3:13).

The New Testament closes with the sublime prayer, "He
who testifies to these things says, 'Yes, I am coming soon.'
Amen. Come, Lord Jesus" (Revelation 22:20).

As we consider the promise of the second coming, we
need to understand that Christ comes in more than one way.
Some of us tend to assume that every New Testament reference to Christ's coming refers to his second coming. However, if we do that, we make a mistake.

Part of the confusion arises from the fact that many
mistakenly interpret the phrases last days or end times as
referring to the time immediately preceding the final return
of Christ. But in fact these phrases describe the entire New
Testament age.

Peter gives a clear example of this when, in order to
explain what occurred on the day of Pentecost, he quotes
from the prophet Joel: "In the last days, God says, I will pour
out my Spirit on all people" (Acts 2:17). Peter is saying that
the events of Pentecost are in fulfillment of Joel 2:28-32,
which is a last-days prophecy. When was it fulfilled? At
Pentecost, the beginning of the New Testament age. "The last
days" is a way to describe the age in which we live.

The Jews spoke of "the former age" and "the last age"
or "the last days." The former age was the time before the
Messiah, the last days the age of the Messiah—the era of the
New Testament church. The writer of Hebrews teaches the
same concept: "But in these last days he has spoken to us by
his Son, whom he appointed heir of all things, and through

whom he made the universe" (Hebrews 1:2). The public ministry of Jesus Christ ushered in the last days.

Because the "coming" of Christ is described in connection with the last days, therefore, it does not invariably allude to the second coming. The Bible teaches a coming of Christ that is not the final coming but is his coming in judgment or deliverance. Christ's direct intervention in our current affairs, in terms either of his vindicating the church by temporal judgments on the unrighteous or of his sending revival and special manifestations of his gracious glory, is referred to as his "coming."

For example: although many apply Matthew 24:1–35 exclusively to the second coming, Christ is in fact primarily depicting the destruction of Jerusalem. True, this act of judgment is a picture and prediction of the comprehensive judgment of the second coming. But isn't it obvious from verses 35 and 36 that the events of verses 1–35 will be fulfilled in that generation, whereas the timing of the events of the final coming is unknown?

> "Heaven and earth will pass away, but my words will never pass away. No one knows about that day or hour, not even the angels in heaven, nor the Son, but only the Father. As it was in the days of Noah, so it will be at the coming of the Son of Man" (Matthew 24:35, 36).

When Christ refers to the suddenness of his coming (vs. 27), we ought to interpret this as his coming to judge the Jewish people for their rejection of the Messiah.

Some people object to this interpretation because of the language of Matthew 24:29: "Immediately after the distress of those days, 'the sun will be darkened, and the moon will not give its light; and stars will fall from the sky, and the heavenly bodies will be shaken.'" They ask, "Was this also fulfilled?" Yes indeed. This is special prophetic language called "apocalyptic language." It is used to describe calamitous acts of judgment. Isaiah uses it to describe the destruction of the Babylonian Empire (Isaiah 13:10). Joel uses it in connection with Pentecost and the overthrowing of the Jewish order (Joel 2:30, 31).

This is not to say that such language has no reference to the second coming. The immediate prediction was of the destruction of the temple; but like many other prophecies, it has a far-ranging fulfillment in temporal judgments throughout the age and ultimately in the final return of Christ.

We may conclude that some references to Christ's coming point to his coming during this age in acts of judgment. In addition to describing acts of temporal judgment, the term refers to Christ's coming in grace. Jesus says to his disciples, "I will not leave you as orphans; I will come to you. . . . If anyone loves me, he will obey my teaching. My Father will love him, and we will come to him and make our home with him" (John 14:18, 23). Christ comes to the church with manifestations of his gracious presence, love, and favor. Thus, not all references to Christ's coming have to do with the second coming. We must study each reference in terms of its context and interpret it accordingly.

However, the great coming of Christ that is prefigured in these other comings, both in judgment and in deliverance, is the second advent. Whereas the term last days refers to the whole New Testament age, there are specific terms that refer to Christ's final coming.

Jesus talks about the day of his return as "that day." "Many will say to me on that day, 'Lord, Lord, did we not prophesy in your name, and in your name drive out demons and perform many miracles?' Then I will tell them plainly, 'I never knew you. Away from me, you evildoers!'" (Matthew 7:22).

The great day of Christ's return is also called "the day" (1 Corinthians 3:3), "the day of the Lord" (1 Thessalonians 5:2) and "the day of judgment" (2 Peter 2:9). These terms refer to the final coming of the Lord—to that great day when Christ puts the period to history and declares, "The End!"

This promise secures the anchor of our hope. Many houses on the seacoast have a "widow's walk" from which the captain's wife daily searched the horizon for a sign of her husband's ship. So we, the bride of Christ, expectantly wait for the Captain of our salvation.

The Events of the Second Coming

When we talk about the return of Christ, the question that preoccupies many is, "What are the events leading up to it? Should we look for certain signs that will alert us to his coming?" There are a number of theories concerning the events surrounding Christ's coming. Many of the theories revolve around the millenial reign of Christ.

The term *millenial* means "one thousand." The different theories are various attempts to interpret what Revelation 20:2 says about Satan's being bound for a thousand years. Historic premillenialism asserts that when Christ comes, he will establish his kingdom upon the earth for a thousand years. During that time the Jews will be converted and many Gentiles as well. Most premillenialists believe in a double resurrection: Christ will raise the righteous when he comes, but the unrighteous will not be raised until the end of his thousand year reign. Many premillenialists also interpret last-day statements as signs of events immediately preceding the return of Christ.

Amillenialists believe that the thousand years began with the resurrection and ascension of Christ. When Christ rose, Satan was bound. The thousand years is a figurative way to describe the New Testament age. During this time good struggles against evil, but very little outside the gathering of the elect will be accomplished.

Postmillenialists apply to the church the Old Testament prophecies about the glory of Zion. The postmillenialist considers the thousand years a time of increased gospel prosperity. The nations will come to a knowledge of the Lord Jesus Christ, and a great number of Jews will be converted. While some postmillenialists agree with amillenialists that the thousand years is the church age, others look for a specific time during the church age—maybe not a literal thousand years, but a specific time—in which the gospel will achieve great victory throughout the world.

Regardless of his millenial view, however, every biblical Christian agrees on the great events surrounding the return of Christ. Paul outlines the major details:

Brothers, we do not want you to be ignorant about those who fall asleep, or to grieve like the rest of men, who have no hope. We believe that Jesus died and rose again and so we believe that God will bring with Jesus those who have fallen asleep in him. According to the Lord's own word, we tell you that we who are still alive, who are left till the coming of the Lord, will certainly not precede those who have fallen asleep. For the Lord himself will come down from heaven, with a loud command, with the voice of the archangel and with the trumpet call of God, and the dead in Christ will rise first. After that, we who are still alive and are left will be caught up together with them in the clouds to meet the Lord in the air. And so we will be with the Lord forever. Therefore encourage each other with these words (1 Thessalonians 4:13–18).

Paul teaches us that Christ's coming will be physical, visible and personal. At a specific moment in history, a great electrifying shout will ring out from heaven. Then, accompanied by his angelic army and the souls of just men made perfect and heralded by the blast of a trumpet, Christ will appear immediately in such a manner that every inhabitant of the earth will see him in a split second.

The second thing Paul teaches is that the dead will be raised and their bodies and souls will be reunited. Their souls will accompany Christ, and at his word the graves will give up their prey. Christ will reunite body and soul. Those who remain alive will be transformed, taken up in the air to meet him. Thus, the resurrected and the transformed will meet in the presence of Christ.

> What are we to believe concerning the resurrection? We are to believe, that at the last day there shall be a general resurrection of the dead, both of the just and unjust, when they that are then found alive shall in a moment be changed; and the self-same bodies of the dead which were laid in the grave, being then again reunited with their souls forever, shall be raised up by the power of Christ. The bodies of the just, by the Spirit of Christ, and by virtue of his resurrection as their head, shall be raised in power, spiritual, incorruptible, and made like to his glorious body; and the bodies of the wicked shall be raised up in dishonor by him, as an offended judge (LC, Q/A 87).

Third, Christ will execute judgment. The Larger Catechism gives the details of judgment:

> What shall immediately follow after the resurrection? Immediately after the resurrection shall follow the general and final judgment of angels and men; the day and hour whereof no man knoweth, that all may watch and pray, and be ever ready for the coming of the Lord (LC, Q/A 88).

All people will be gathered before him. The righteous will be on Christ's right and the unrighteous on his left (Matthew 25:33). On the day of judgment no one will be held in suspense awaiting the outcome. In fact, the righteous will sit with the Lord in judgment upon the reprobate.

Finally, when the judgment is finished, the Lord Jesus Christ will hand the mediatorial kingdom over to God the Father. "Then the end will come, when he hands over the kingdom to God the Father after he has destroyed all dominion, authority and power. For he must reign until he has put all his enemies under his feet" (1 Corinthians 15:24, 25). Elect angels and redeemed people will live with the triune God forever in the bliss of perfect fellowship.

When the Bible speaks of these great events, it does not emphasize signs but rather the suddenness and unexpectedness of Christ's return. We are to live with a consciousness that the Lord is coming. We ought to live with an awareness of our short life span, particularly in comparison to eternity and God's purposes. We must be prepared for his coming for us personally in our death or coming for us corporately at his second coming.

This means that we are to live as faithful stewards who will give an accounting for the deeds done in the flesh (Matthew 24:45–25:30). We must be faithful and not negligent or lethargic in the responsibilities he has given to us.

Furthermore, the doctrine of Christ's second coming gives strength and comfort. God fortifies us as we meditate on the truth of Christ's final return. For the time being, we suffer and struggle with sin, with our infirmities, and with Satan and all those who follow him. But Christ is coming. He will deliver and vindicate. He will make all things well.

Each of us ought to long to be with Christ and to see the church vindicated and made perfect. It will be a glorious day when sin is eradicated once for all and we will praise God with unfettered strength and devotion.

Moreover, we are comforted in the midst of our grief for lost loved ones who were Christians. True, death is unnatural. We should not be separated from them. It tears us up. But Paul reminds us that we should not grieve as those who have no hope (1 Thessalonians 4:13). Christ will return, and the dead will be raised. Then there will be the greatest family reunion ever. Thus, Paul concludes his discussion of Christ's return, "Therefore encourage each other with these words" (1 Thessalonians 4:18).

THE END!

Christ is coming. Amen. Come, Lord Jesus.

Review Questions

1. What is the last act of Christ's exaltation?

2. What period is meant by the phrases *last days* and *end times*?

3. In what two ways does Christ come during the last days?

4. What terms does the Bible use to refer to the time of Christ's second coming?

5. State the three millenial views.

6. List the events involved in Christ's final return.

7. How should knowledge of Christ's return effect us as Christians?

Discussion Questions

1. How does one's eschatology affect his approach to church life and service? his attitude to work? his attempts to bring godly changes to society?

2. According to 2 Corinthians 5:10, 11, how does Christ's return relate to the fear of God?

3. Discuss the pros and cons of the three millenial views.

Appendix A

THE NICENE CREED

I Believe in one God, the Father Almighty, Maker of heaven and earth, And of all things visible and invisible.

And in one Lord Jesus Christ, the Only-begotten Son of God, Begotten of His Father before all worlds, God of God, Light of Light, Very God of very God, Begotten not made, Being of one substance with the Father, By Whom all things were made; Who, for us men, and for our salvation, came down from heaven, And was incarnate by the Holy Ghost of the Virgin Mary, And was made man; And was crucified also for us under Pontius Pilate. He suffered and was buried; and the third day He rose again, according to the Scriptures; And ascended into heaven, And sitteth on the right hand of the Father; And He shall come again with glory to judge both the quick and the dead; Whose kingdom shall have no end.

And I believe in the Holy Ghost, The Lord and Giver of Life, Who proceedeth from the Father and the Son, Who with the Father and the Son together is worshipped and glorified, Who spake by the Prophets. And I believe in one holy Christian and Apostolic Church. I acknowledge one Baptism for the remission of sins; And I look for the Resurrection of the dead; And the Life of the world to come. Amen.

Appendix B

THE CHALCEDONIAN FORMULA

Following the holy fathers, we all unanimously teach that one and same Son, our Lord Jesus Christ, is to be confessed:

Perfect in Deity and perfect in Humanity,
Truly God and truly Man,
Of a rational soul and body,
Consubstantial with the Father according to his Deity,
Consubstantial with us according to his Humanity,
Like us in all respects, apart from sin;
Before the ages begotten of the Father according to his
    Deity,
And in these last days for us and for our salvation was
    born of the Virgin Mary, the Mother of God according
    to his Humanity,
One and the same Christ, Son, Lord, only-begotten,
To be acknowledged in Two Natures
    without confusion or change
    without division or separation;
The difference in the Natures being by no means removed
    by the union,
but rather the property of each Nature being preserved
    and concurring in one Person and one Subsistence,
Not parted or divided into two Persons,
but one and the same Son and Only-begotten, God the
    Word, the Lord Jesus Christ;
According as at first the prophets, then the Lord Jesus
    Christ himself, taught us concerning him,
And as the Creed of the fathers has handed down to us.